The Employer Safety Guidebook

to

Zero Employee Injury

by
Emmitt J. Nelson, P.E.

The Zero Injury Guide Book

Zero Employee Injury
March 2003

Published by:

Nelson Consulting, Inc.
10031 Briar Drive
Houston, Texas 77042

Copyright © 2002 by Emmitt J. Nelson, P.E.

All rights reserved under International Copyright Conventions.

Printed in the United States of America

ISBN 09664896-3-2

First Edition

The Zero Injury Guide Book

APPRECIATION

Writing a book is a long term project. Parts of this book have been in process for at least 20 years. The work in its present form has not made it to press before now for many reasons, but I feel it can wait no longer. It is clear that it has been greatly enhanced by the material made available since its inception and can clearly be a much more powerful contribution to the business world now than had it been published in a prior year.

I owe a large debt of gratitude to many of my industrial colleagues, both in Shell Oil Company and others who, sometimes unwittingly, but powerfully impacted the content of this effort through their many encouragements as we have walked this path of bringing the Zero Injury message to the construction industry in particular and along with this to companies at large no matter their business enterprise.

My thanks also goes to Dr. Richard L. Tucker, currently occupant, Joe C. Walter Chair in Engineering, The University of Texas, Austin, for his in-depth critique and recommendations on a host of matters pertaining to the content and presentation of this work.

Also my deepest gratitude goes to my wife Ginny for her unfailing encouragement and to our Granddaughter Christina Ashie, an Honors English student, for her untiring editing. If flaws remain in this book they are caused by my failings and not these who have selflessly made their earnest contribution to its success.

Four construction industry colleagues volunteered to read and comment on the manuscript. I wish to thank them all. Excerpts from their comments may be seen on the back cover.

Emmitt J. Nelson, P.E.

The Zero Injury Guide Book

ABOUT THE AUTHOR

Emmitt J. Nelson has been in the safety consulting business since retirement from Shell Oil Company in 1989. Prior to and since retirement he has authored and co-authored a number of articles for trade magazines on construction safety management. During the final five years of his career with Shell Oil Company he led a corporate emphasis on bringing contractor safety performance into line with Shell's own employee's safety performance. This required leading in the creation of a corporate-wide contractor safety strategy. The results were realized in significantly reduced injury to contractor employees, lower contractor's Workers' Compensation Insurance costs and increased profits for the contractors and more competitive bidding on Shell projects.

Immediately upon retirement from Shell, employers interested in reducing injury to their employees enlisted Emmitt as a consultant. He founded Nelson Consulting, Incorporated, in 1992, a Texas Corporation specializing in teaching the Zero Injury concept. He leads clients in the installation of the safety management processes required to create a zero injury working culture. The best of his clients achieve 1,000,000 work hours with zero Recordables.

The author is a B.S. graduate in Mechanical Engineering from Texas A&M University, and a Registered Professional Engineer in the State of Texas. He was honored for his industry wide safety contribution in the year 2000 by being elected to membership in The National Academy of Construction.

While with Shell Oil Company, he was Shell's representative on the Business Roundtable Construction Committee where he served as Chairman in 1988. Additionally during 1987 and 1988 he served as Co-Chairman of The Center for Construction Education, located at Texas A&M University. He also served as Chairman of the Construction Industry Institute Zero Accidents Taskforce from 1990 to 1993. This Taskforce performed research into the Zero Injury phenomenon uncovering the safety management strategies used by those employers who are successful in working millions of hours with Zero Accidents.

In this book, written to benefit employers of all kinds, he explains how a dedicated and committed employer can lead their organization in a safety culture change where injury to employees is a very rare event.

The Zero Injury Guide Book

PREFACE – by Dr. Richard L. Tucker, Joe C. Walter, Jr. Chair in Engineering, The University of Texas, Austin

I am honored to provide my perspective on "The Employer Safety Guidebook to Zero Employee Injury." Perhaps a bit of history will be useful in providing the context of this important work.

While I served as the Founding Director of the Construction Industry Institute, a research organization involving many of our nation's largest owners, contractors and universities, the concept of Zero Accidents came into being. CII was itself a pioneer effort and, in its early days, its industry representatives met regularly to identify important research areas. At one of these meetings, Keith Price, Executive Vice-President of Morrison-Knudson, stated "We need to address construction safety. We must find ways to reduce injuries on our job sites." Thus, CII began its safety research studies in the mid-1980's. Expectations were modest, since the industry's safety statistics had not improved for many years.

Emmitt and I were not well acquainted at that time, and he was not involved in the initial CII safety research. As representative for Shell Oil Company, he was elected as Chairman of the Business Roundtable's Construction Committee, an organization known for its earlier "Construction Industry Cost Effectiveness Project." With the support of John Bookout, CEO of Shell Oil Company, the Business Roundtable Construction Committee, under the Directorship of Richard F. Kibben, launched a major safety initiative. That initiative, built around safety excellence awards and recognition, for owners and contractors, significantly raised the visibility of safety in the owner community. As this effort progressed, Emmitt's passion for safety improvement became increasingly obvious. He retired from Shell Oil Company after completing his term as chairman of the Construction Committee, but continued his drive for safety improvements as a safety management consultant.

Shortly after Emmitt's retirement, the CII began considering additional safety research. It even set goals for safety improvements for its companies to achieve by the year 2000. (The goals were modest; only a 25% improvement.) At one of the CII Board of Advisors meetings, a member stated "We must find ways to eliminate all accidents on our job sites. Only zero accidents is acceptable!" Thus, a name and charge were born for a new research effort. I then contacted Jim Braus, a Shell executive, and asked if the company might re-hire Emmitt, as a consultant, to lead the Zero Accidents Research Team. Shell readily agreed.

The Zero Injury Guide Book

As they say, "the rest is history." Emmitt's passion was shared by the other team members. They brainstormed and formulated ways to generate a "zero accidents" mentality throughout the industry. I felt that some of their ideas were impractical and cautioned against their implementation. They didn't take my advice, and they were right. The CII videotape, "One Too Many" and its associated Zero Injury publications rapidly became CII's most widely adopted products. Many CII member company safety records improved dramatically, as illustrated in this book.

Emmitt's devotion to Zero Injury in employee safety continues. He is one of our industry's most noted safety consultants and has been recognized by election to the National Academy of Construction. This book will not be the culmination of his efforts, because he will continue to be active. However, it provides a seminal contribution to our drive for safety improvements.

<u>It is possible to have zero accidents, and this Guidebook tells us how!</u>

Richard L. Tucker
September 19, 2002

The Zero Injury Guide Book

INTRODUCTION BY AUTHOR

It was in 1987 that The Business Roundtable Construction Committee gave the first Construction Industry Safety Excellence awards. It was noted that two of the awardees, an owner and a contractor, had performed their work without Lost Workday cases for two years and four years respectively. These amazing achievements for that time were soon labeled the "Zero Injury" phenomenon borrowing from author Philip Crosby's "Zero Defect" approach to Quality.

The significance of this zero lost workday case performance was most startling when compared to the OSHA National Averages for worker injury in construction in the year 1986 of 6.8 lost workday cases per 100 workers. Comparing the OSHA national average to these awardees that worked a combined 6.8 million work-hours with no Lost Workday Cases, the two companies avoided 231 serious injuries to their workers. Wow!

When these achievements were announced by the Business Roundtable many asked, "How do they do that?"

Soon after, the Construction Industry Institute (CII), located in Austin, Texas, and led by Dr. Richard L. Tucker, agreed to commission a research Taskforce to look into the question of: "How do some contractors and owners achieve millions of hours worked in construction without serious injury?"

The research performed by the "Zero Accident Taskforce" was completed in 1993. In 1999 CII decided to follow-up with an investigation of recent reports about projects completing with "Zero Recordable" achievements; an even more amazing safety performance than "Zero Lost Workday Cases" investigated in 1993. Their research, reported in 2001 and 2002, verified and expanded on the 1993 results yielding additional quantifiable data that reflects significant safety performance improvements in companies that have utilized and improved upon the original Zero Injury techniques. Many of these have achieved Zero Recordables for extended numbers of work hours. The CII "Making Zero Injury a Reality" Task Force restated the injury original five critical safety elements, increasing the number from five techniques to nine.

This Employer Safety Guidebook describes the successful application of the CII research derived Zero Employee Injury safety management techniques and introduces a safety management process that helps achieve the most critical aspects of creating a working culture and process where employee injury is rare.

The Zero Injury Guide Book

TABLE OF CONTENTS

	Page
APPRECIATION	3
ABOUT THE AUTHOR	4
PREFACE by Dr. Richard L. Tucker	6
INTRODUCTION	7

PART ONE –
In-depth look at Zero Injury — 9
1. THE SEARCH FOR ZERO INJURY — 10
2. DEFINING ZERO INJURY — 17
3. THE LOGIC BEHIND THE ZERO INJURY CONCEPT — 20
4. THE ZERO INJURY RESEARCH - IN SUMMARY — 32
5. CORPORATE LEADERSHIP IS REQUIRED — 37
6. INJURY RATES AND THE COST OF INJURY — 42
7. ZERO INJURY RETURN ON INVESTMENT — 50
8. REDEFINING SAFETY COMMITMENT — 57
9. THE 1993 CONSTRUCTION INDUSTRY INSTITUTE RESEARCH - IN DETAIL — 63
10. THE 2001/2002 CONSTRUCTION INDUSTRY INSTITUTE RESEARCH - IN DETAIL — 70
11. AUTHOR'S RECOMMENDATIONS — 82

PART TWO –
The Continuous Improvement Process — 87
12. TAKING MANAGEMENT ACTION — 88
13. THE PROCESS THAT YIELDS SAFETY PROGRESS — 91
14. SAFETY MANAGEMENT SYSTEM EVOLUTION — 96
15. SAFETY MANAGEMENT CHOICES — 98
16. THE SAFETY MANAGEMENT SYSTEM — 101
17. SAFETY TEAMS — 129
18. MANAGING THE SYSTEM — 134

PART THREE –
Appendix — 137
ITEM 1 SOPHISTICATED SAFETY TEAMS — 140
ITEM 2 TREATISE ON MONETARY INCENTIVES — 166
ITEM 3 ZERO INJURY TECHNIQUES EXPLAINED — 177
ITEM 4 ZERO INJURY RETURN ON INVESTMENT — 193
REFERENCES — 199
INDEX — 202

PART 1

AN IN-DEPTH EXPLANATION OF THE ZERO INJURY CONCEPT

Chapter 1 - The Search for Zero Injury
The Illusive Dream!

Safety Excellence Defined
The Search for Zero Injury; where is the trailhead; where do we start; do you have a map?

The answer to these questions is right here in this Guide Book; the "trailhead" begins here; you have the map in your hands!

Take a look!

In recent times, the words "Zero Injury" has come to mean that long sought superior competitive safety performance that enlightened leaders wish to lead their organizations to achieve.

In much of American industry, the decade of the 1990's was spent in pursuit of safety excellence. I predict the decade of 2001-10 will be one where "those that are still seeking" pursuing those "that have found" the keys to a Zero Injury workplace. Many people in business and industry struggle with defining their personal answer to the following two questions.

What is safety excellence? Can it be defined?

A good definition of safety excellence is this.

> *"A company or group of employees have reached safety excellence when all 'at-risk behavior' has been eliminated."*

In contrast, however, repeatedly the definition of "safety excellence" commonly found in business and industry is as varied as there are companies. Too often leaders accept mediocrity (always un-intentioned) as their definition of safety excellence.

All too many say to themselves, "Not to worry, we are doing everything we can. After all, we are better than the OSHA/BLS national average." Or those above the national average might say, "If we can just get our performance in line with the national average we will be fine."

Since an "OSHA/BLS average" is the arithmetically combined and normalized safety statistics of all in an industry group there are those below average and there are those above average. It is commonly found that in any industry group there are at least a few companies that experience no injuries for the entire data year. Zero!

Despite this, it seems the approach most executives take in measuring their own company's safety performance is to compare their data with the average. As they do this, more often than not, they do not even stop to realize that there are those in their industrial group without an injury. They perform at Zero Injury!

Why settle for the average? Why don't we measure our performance against the best: those with no injuries?

Here, the key questions should be, "Who are they, and how do they accomplish such performance?"

This Guide Book Reveals
What I am going to do in this Guide Book is to identify who these successful companies are in one industry, the construction industry, and exactly how they are attaining such lofty performance levels.

Of course this objective will cause those not in the

construction industry to ask, "Why should I read what those in the construction are doing when I am in a different industry?"

The answer is simply that employee safety is a people management issue. While the hazards presented in various industries are different, the people are the same. Copy what these in construction are doing in managing safety with their people and you, too, can achieve Zero Injury.

Safety: A Psychological Game
While I do not view safety as a "game" the phrase application applies. No matter the industry, above all else safety in the workplace is a mental game, a thinking game or "mental safety" if you prefer.

How many times have you heard after an injury a statement by the injured like the following? "I just wasn't thinking."

How many times have you heard leaders say, "If we could just get everyone to be on the alert and mentally engaged in their own safety all the time we would be OK."

Such a view of "mental safety" gives significant insight into the principal challenge faced in creating a working culture where "risk taking" is a rare event. In the realm of "mental safety," there is an additional aspect to be addressed. In addition to the first, the "thinking element" there is also the second, the "knowing element."

Here, I am simply saying that, in practicing safety an employee cannot think of something they do not know; thus, as far as safety training is concerned, employees are unable to think of some of the "at-risk" behaviors they have not been trained to avoid.

To create the possibility of Zero Injury there are two primary challenges remaining after the safety training is complete. These challenges are 'motivational." While training is of paramount importance and is an absolute requirement for a sound safety program, motivating employees to (1) "think safe" and to (2) "follow that safe thinking" with "safe behavior" is the bottom line challenge all, management and worker alike, face in creating a workplace free of injury.

As an example, while speaking recently with the safety director of a construction firm that had just exceeded 2,500,000 work-hours (August 2001) with Zero Recordable injuries, he made the following simple observation.

"After one has implemented all the key zero injury safety management techniques, success in achieving a zero injury workplace is 99.9% between the ears. Believing you can is critical. Too many people do not believe they can achieve such lofty dreams," he said. Continuing he said, "The simplicity of my point was illustrated to me in the first grade by the story about the little Steam Engine that puffed up the hill with the monologue 'I think I can, I think I can, I think I can, I know I can.'" He added, "If people insist they cannot work injury free they will not."

<u>It's a Culture Change</u>
How does an organization go about changing the work culture to one where there is little "at-risk" behavior?

In a historic work culture, while injury is not wanted and all people work to prevent injury, nonetheless, when an injury occurs, the injury event all too often is treated as though it were inevitable! "Injuries do occur, after all" is the thought in everyone's mind.

Please allow me to advance an observation that is essential to a Zero Injury culture.

The Zero Injury Guide Book

The fact that injuries do occur, does not mean that injuries must occur.

In analyzing "most all injuries" there is discovered a number of interventions that if accomplished would have prevented the injury.

To illustrate this point allow me to give an example. A client found in investigating a fatality, an in-depth analysis of the events leading up to the death uncovered seven potential accident intervention actions. If any one of these seven preventive actions leading to the event, been taken, the fatality would likely not occurred.

You may have noticed two paragraphs above, I used the term "most all injuries." The use of these words recognizes that "on occasion" injuries may result from an "act of God," such as a sudden windstorm or a lightning bolt.

In such cases one can be on the alert and remove themselves from areas of maximum exposure to minimize the chance of being injured.

By way of observation too many people overuse the term "act of God." Some would say that if a machine fails leading to an injury such a failure was an "act of God." As an engineer, trained in equipment design, I disagree. For instance, if a machine is being used in such a way that the possibility of failure exists, then it is incumbent on management to remove the possibility of a failure, or to remove the possibility of a failure causing injury. Machine guarding is a common example of the latter.

The key point I am making in the paragraphs above is the following observation:

The Zero Injury Guide Book

The common enemy of a safe work culture is "in the mind" of company leaders, managers, foremen, union leaders and workers.

One could say that the possibility of working injury free is "locked behind the prison bars of tradition."

Based on past traditional experience the thinking is, "since injuries have always occurred then it is a given; injuries will occur." This is both truth and fallacy! While it is true an injury will occur someday, those who achieve Zero Injury work with the simple commitment that "we will prevent all injury today." It is a fallacy to think that an injury cannot be prevented.

As this fallacy becomes entrenched in our belief system, the inadvertent "mind-set" for many becomes: "I know injuries will occur. Beyond a nominal amount of effort to encourage the use of safe behavior on the part of the worker and complying with all legal requirements there is little 'else' to be done by those in charge."

With this mind-set, failure is inevitable, and accepted even before beginning the effort to address the subject of Zero Injury.

To have a Zero Injury workplace, this "injuries will occur" mind-set must be challenged and changed.

And here is the good news.

Repeatedly, research has proven there is something "else" that can be done. It is found in embracing a new "mind-set" or "concept" on how to manage safety.

Many who successfully use the Zero Injury approach call it the "Zero Injury Concept" of safety management. When applied, a company or project culture change is required and sought. The culture of accepting injury, as a product of our business must change to one where all employees, from the worker to the CEO, believe that injury can be prevented and all accept that challenge.

The Zero Injury safety management concept was not invented by this author but was invented by employers who dared to think the seemingly impossible.

A commitment to the Zero Injury Concept, simply stated, is: "Since no one wants an injury to occur and since any injury causes our employee to suffer and also harms our business plan <u>we will do whatever it takes</u> to prevent the injury of our employees."

The Zero Injury Guide Book

Chapter 2 – Defining Zero Injury

Defining The Zero Injury Concept

To begin this pursuit of a Zero Injury safety culture change, first allow me to define the term "Zero Injury."

Many people ask me if in using the term Zero Injury I mean that there can be absolutely "zero injury?"

In applying the basic Zero Injury Concept the answer is a clear yes. That is the concept. No injuries of any kind whatsoever! Zero!

At this point again the skeptics think such is impossible.

My simple reply is as follows:

"It is not impossible. You are already achieving Zero Injury. Unless an employer has an injury to one of their employees every day, some days are performed at the Zero Injury rate."

The question is not: "Is Zero Injury possible?" but rather is "How long can my group of employees work without an injury of any kind?"

Allow me to illustrate. Say you have a group of 100 employees. (This is a handy number to use because OSHA measures injury frequency using a cohort of 100 employees.)

For this example let's take the manufacturing industry in America. OSHA reports that in 2001 there were an average of 8.1 OSHA Recordable Injuries per 100 workers. This means that in 200,000 work-hours 8+ injuries occurred.

Where do the 200,000 work-hours hours come from? Why use that standard to measure?

The Zero Injury Guide Book

It is 100 employees working eight hours per day for 250 days. 100 x 8 x 250 = 200,000.

Where does the 250 days come from?

It is 365 days less 102 weekend days less about 10 to 12 holidays. The result is approximately 250 days; give or take a day or two.

Getting back to our 8.1 injuries in 200,000 work-hour analyses, if 200,000 work-hours occur in 250 days what do we get if we divide 8.1 injuries into 250 workdays? The answer is 30.86 days.

Thus in 2001, as an average, one hundred manufacturing employees worked 30.86 days between Recordable injuries. This means that for a period of near 31 days there were Zero Recordable injuries. This same rate in 1989 was only about 16 days, a big improvement.

So there you have it!

Zero Injury is already being achieved! You see, unless all employers have one injury every day, then some are working some days at Zero Injury. The question is, "can a manufacturing employer beat the national average and by how much?"

Since 8.1 is an average, and since some are better the average and some are worse than the average, the answer is a clear "yes" for beating the average. Some do.

The Zero Injury Concept applied in your company will allow you to achieve safety performance 5 to 10 times better than the national average. In construction some have achieved results 30 times better than the national average in work where injury rates are also very high.

Some have worked over 2,000,000 hours with zero recordable injury! This is equivalent to 100 employees working 10 years with no recordable injuries. Quite remarkable, I say!

Regarding the above example, the obvious question is, "Does your company measure how many days, or work-hours you work between recordable injuries?"

Most employers do not.

All employee groups work some number of total hours between injuries, whether that injury is a First Aid Case, a Recordable or a Lost Workday Case. So, as a first step, I urge you to begin to measure total hours worked between injuries. Then compare your result of how you are doing to the OSHA/BLS national average for your industry. Adopt and use the zero injury research information and commit to improve until you too join those who have achieved world-class safety performance.

An "often unasked" question regarding Zero Injury is: "Could you give me the logic behind this Zero Injury approach because it seems so unbelievable?"

Read the next chapter for your answer!

The Zero Injury Guide Book

Chapter 3 – The Logic Behind the Zero Injury Concept

<u>Who wants an Injury?</u>
The first question in the logic test is -

"Who wants an injury to occur?"

The answer, of course, is "No one!"

Not the worker, not the worker's family, not the employer company's client, not the company's owner, not the CEO, not the company management, not the worker's supervision, not the worker's co-workers, not the union if the worker is represented, not the community and not government. All are for Zero Injury!

So what is the problem?

The problem, I believe, is found in our past and it seems that some are not willing to change. We look at our past and see the helplessness we have felt in trying to reduce injury. With a glimmer of hope we ask; "How can it be possible that some companies work for millions of hours without recordable injuries? If they, in truth, are doing this and with 'no-one' wanting an injury, why do we not adopt this position also? And work to make it happen rather than accepting the 'status quo?'"

What are some of the issues to be addressed in changing?"

Setting goals allowing for some number of injuries is one of the "status quo" problems.

Believing Zero Injury cannot be accomplished is one of the "status quo" problems.

Doubting the numbers of those who are successful in eliminating injury for remarkable periods of time is one of the "status quo" problems.

Want to get out of the "status quo?"

<u>The Logic Against Setting Injury Goals above "Zero"</u>
Second in the logic test is the following question.

"Why not set goals for injury as long as they are stretch goals?"

In my experience some people like to argue that it is unrealistic for the injury commitment to be to "Zero." "After all," they argue, "we have always had injuries and injuries will continue to happen. So to set a Zero Injury commitment flies in the face of reality."

The "goal setting" doubters claim that: "In all reality, injuries will occur, after all, employees are people and they will not follow the safety rules all the time. Therefore we are being very realistic when we set goals for injuries."

Such logic is critically flawed. Allow me to illustrate why.

Let's say you own a small company with 100 employees. Last year your employees experienced five serious lost workday cases. The cost was high, but more importantly you saw the misery and suffering that followed those injuries and as the owner you vowed to do something about it. After consultation with your leaders you decided to set a goal for the year upcoming of only two lost workday cases.

So you gathered all the employees into a safety meeting. On the agenda was your announcement that you were very concerned, that last year there were five lost workday cases and you wanted them all to know that as the owner you were setting a goal for the following year of only two lost workday cases. All your people were enthusiastic and seemed to buy in on the goal of two.

Question: On the first workday in January of your new fiscal year, how many of your 100 employees think, as far as you and the goal is concerned, it is OK for them to have an injury that results in a lost workday case?

The answer is, of course, all 100. Each worker thinks that as long as the goal of two is not reached it is OK for a serious injury to occur! And each employee knows, in reality, that one of those injuries can be his or hers should they be so unfortunate!

What has the goal of "two" done inadvertently? The goal of "two" has said that it is OK for injuries to occur as long as there are no more than two! Not at all the "lets stop injury message" the owner was trying to give the employees.

Now, lets take the scenario further. Say that everyone buckles down and indeed your employees work all the way to July without a serious injury: much better than last year. But an injury does occur in July. Now all of a sudden the goal is no longer two but one! Everyone works even harder. Then as "bad luck would have it" another injury occurs in October. Tough times, the goal of two is now all used up.

Question: What is to be the goal for November and December? Zero?

That is correct; Zero has to be the goal for November and December unless you want to change the goal now that it was not reached. Not a likely choice!

Is it OK for the goal to be zero in November? Of course it is!

If your answer is yes as is mine, then answer this; "Why is it not also OK to have a commitment for the entire year of "zero" beginning in January?"

"Zero Injury" Obviated by Setting Injury Goals

Based on the above logic, I believe a "no injury performance" result is virtually obviated by the common process of setting goals for injury. For when company leaders set goals that allow for some number of injuries; these goals are set, perhaps inadvertently, acknowledging and thereby accepting that a certain number of injuries will be OK should they occur.

When employees acknowledge these goals there also comes the subtle message to all the company employees that injury is permissible and injury up to this goal number is OK as long as the goal number is not exceeded. This subtle message becomes a powerful enemy of creating a Zero Injury safety culture because it allows all employees including the CEO the latitude to sacrifice safety in small ways, (perhaps sub-consciously) always in the interest of production, schedule or cost as long as the injury goal is not exceeded.

As a result, all employees have a psychological message from the hidden thought that, "As long as the company has not reached our goal for injuries, if I were injured today, my injury would not cause us to go over our goal; therefore my injury would be OK."

Such a hidden and subconscious mind-set undermines the very condition management is seeking: the cultural platform where everyone, energetically, focuses their attention on a continuing basis on eliminating unsafe behavior, thus avoiding all injury.

In contrast to setting goals for injury, what is so powerful about the "no injury is acceptable" company position?

Leadership in Safety

I believe Leadership in safety contains five elements.

First, a leader must have the vision of a zero injury result.

Second, a leader must be able to pass that vision on to those being led.

Third, a leader must have the discernment to staff managerial positions with people who have the capability to lead their group to accomplish the vision.

Fourth, a leader must be tenacious in achieving the vision.

Fifth, the leader must have visible integrity in leading the Zero Injury commitment.

When the top company leader sincerely makes the "no injury is acceptable" commitment to safety and communicates that statement to all employees, an expected result can come: success!

Success comes, however, only if lower management buys-in and reinforces the CEO's commitment. Along with the above, when the monetary support appears for safety training, safety procedure development, and implementation of the CII Zero Injury safety techniques required to make it happen, it begins to happen.

With such a "money where your mouth is" approach the employees begin to believe that, at least for this company, the management commitment is far more than "lip service." Employees see management "walking the talk" daily as they support their safety needs in an example setting manner.

When the employees see this consistency it is then that they, too, become believers and they can, with this strong management support, take all the necessary steps to avoid injury.

Further, in a Zero Injury culture, the employees are not badgered by supervision about meeting schedule at the expense of safety; to do so creates the possibility of an injury.

And supervision knows that an injury is tolerated even less than a broken schedule.

Safety as a Core Value
Thus, it becomes apparent to everyone that the CEO/COO is very serious when the critical step comes and the Leader announces, "injury is unacceptable," that "safety is a core value rather than Priority One." Core values do not fall victim to priorities; they describe who you are. Values are those moral absolutes that are the principal driving forces that work production planning is built upon.

As line management consistently acts out this message, the company middle management and the hourly personnel, knowing they are going to have to answer to the CEO if an injury occurs, are then free to place total support behind eliminating the unsafe behavior that leads to injury.

Management employees, who would have argued against a given safety procedure that was giving them a production problem, now quickly agree on the proper and safer course of action and move on. Why?

It is the corporate expectation, and no one wants to be found lacking in supporting safety should an injury result. Such companies become our examples for the definition of the word "commitment." See Chapter 8.

It is in these companies that all employees know that success in the prevention of injury is esteemed above all the other means of success measurement; i.e., cost, schedule, profit margin. It is also in these companies that competitive edge and profit improve!

Zero is the correct approach.
A corporate commitment to Zero Injury sends a distinct and unmistakable message to all employees that any injury is unacceptable. Note also that:

Such a commitment does not undermine the psychology of those in the workplace as all look to work to accomplish that which all want anyway: Zero Injuries.

Such a commitment raises the expected performance standard for all, supervision and workers alike.

Such a commitment eliminates all discussion in the field about "how safe we need to be to achieve zero injury."

Such a commitment allows all to work together to achieve world-class safety rather than simply an amount better than the National Average.

Think about this; we managers must do something different if we are to expect different results. The following is a paraphrase of a statement made by Joe Juran, the Total Quality Guru, defining "insanity."
"Doing the same thing in the same way year after year and expecting different results."

The workplaces of the world are begging for a new approach to worker safety! The logic of taking a commitment to zero injury is being proven by dozens of companies worldwide.

These are the leaders; the starting place for your new safety culture to come into being is to emulate these leaders.

Management must lead in this revolution in safety.

A new dream has been born.

Are you going to take part?

One day at a time.
Work forces in the thousands have always been able to work an eight-hour day without injury to a worker; or even a week, or perhaps a month or two. The Zero Injury concept is nothing more than asking a work force to work injury free "one day at a time" for an extended period.

How long, you ask?

The national average for days worked in construction with a crew of 100 workers without a Lost Workday Case in 2001 was 62 workdays. In 1989 this number was 37 workdays.

Since then the rate of injury has slowly decreased from 6.8 per 100 workers per year to 4.0 per 100. The 62 workdays between Lost Workday Cases for a crew of 100 workers reflects significant improved safety performance in the construction industry over the period.

The following is how the number of days is calculated. The Recordable Rate will be used in the illustration.

The BLS/OSHA Recordable Incident rate in construction was 7.9 for 2001.

With the 7.9 rate for 100 workers the days between injury calculation is -

$$\text{Days} = \frac{100 \text{ workers} \times 2000 \text{ hours per year}}{7.9 \text{ Injuries} \times 800 \text{ hours per day}} = 31.65 \text{ days}$$

This average is 14.17 days better than it was in 1989 when the average was 17.48 days.

Companies that have committed themselves to a Zero Injury safety culture are contributing a large part of this improvement.

The Real Truth
During the 20th Century the real truth was that the principal emphasis on worker safety on the job was to "try" to work injury free. I put quotes on the word "try" to explain that was a "small emphasis" by today's standard at the beginning of the 20th Century. That "small emphasis" grew to a "large emphasis" by the end of the Century actually passing into the 21st Century at the end of the day December 31, 2000.

While achieving Zero Lost Workday Cases was the principle focus during the past 20 years, the effort is now focusing more and more on achieving Zero Recordable injuries. The best records in construction now run to over 2,500,000 Recordable free hours. To get a perspective on the significance of 2,000,000 work-hours think of the milestone this way: Two million hours is equivalent to a "workdays between recordable injuries" rate for 100 workers of 10 years (2500 work days). This is nothing less than an amazing accomplishment. Quite a contrast to the 2001 OSHA/BLS National average for construction of 31 days, wouldn't you say?

Now there are many more at the beginning of the 21st century that are achieving as many as 1,000,000 hours with Zero Recordable injuries.

These are the world trendsetters, the best of the best. They are the best of the Zero Injury believers and achievers!

Believability
Some people like to doubt the zero injury data coming out of the construction industry. However, I stoutly maintain the data are valid. In proof all I can say is that it is very hard, to even impossible, to keep several dozen seriously injured and maimed employees hidden on a large construction project. Look around on these jobs. Talk to the employees; if they give testimony to the truth of the data, it is true.

Unfortunately, one has to recognize that there may be a few who do "play games" with the injury record keeping. These are only kidding themselves. Record keeping integrity is mandatory for a Zero Injury work culture to exist. If the employees see "game playing" with the recording of injury, management loses the worker support so vital to a true Zero Injury culture. But, thankfully, these that manipulate injury record keeping are in a minority.

Construction worker safety in the 21st Century is being pursued in unique and admirable ways. The real truth is, "worker injury has experienced a dramatic reduction through the use of the Construction Industry Institute's Zero Injury research results."

The Leading Examples
The good news is that there are hundreds of employers today who have embraced the notion "that injuries do not have to occur," and they have learned how to intervene. Their combined performance is nothing short of remarkable when compared to the OSHA/BLS National Averages for injury in the workplace.

The Zero Injury Guide Book

Allow me to give some examples of Zero Injury performance. I frame these examples with a question, "Would you believe me if I told you that in the decade of the 1990's...?"

Would you believe me if I told you that H.B Zachry, Inc., of San Antonio, Texas while performing construction work for Shell Chemical, at Norco, Louisiana, worked over 1,200,000 work-hours without a single OSHA Recordable Injury early in the 1990 decade?

Would you believe me if I told you that a contractor, Fluor-Daniel, Irvine, California, performing construction for CITGO in Lake Charles, Louisiana worked a total of 2,080,000 work-hours without a single OSHA Recordable in mid-decade?

Would you believe me if I told you that in August, 2001, Cherne Construction, a Minneapolis, MN, "union only" contractor surpassed 2,500,000 direct hire work-hours with Zero Recordables.

Would you believe me if I told you that S&B Engineering and Construction, located in Houston, Texas, as of Jan. 2003 are running a string of 31,000,000 hours without a single Lost Workday Case. Their previous LW Case occurred in 1996. Would you believe me if I told you that this same contractor's Piping Department worked over 1,000,000 hours without an OSHA Recordable.

Would you believe me if I told you that Day and Zimmerman, a Pennsylvania contractor, worked a string of 1,000,000 hours on one of their projects without a single OSHA Recordable Injury?

Examples from overseas are also available. It is recognized that comparing North American data and overseas data should be done with specific knowledge of the working cultures in these overseas countries. It is not an "apples versus apples" comparison. Many times the average workers are "ex-pats" and are supporting family back in their home country and, most of all, they do not "want" to be injured. In working for contractors who aggressively support that "want," they are successful.

In any case, lets look at one worthy project. Would you believe me if I told you of a 1.2 billion dollar project in Saudi Arabia that completed 25,000,000 hours with only one Lost Workday Case? And, at one point in the project, all the contractor's combined data ran a string of 14,000,000 hours with Zero Recordables? Would you believe me if I told you, that one of the three principal contractors on the project, amassed 12.5 million hours with Zero Recordables?

The above are but the leading examples. There are many more employers in construction, recognized as a hazardous occupation, that manage their worker safety effort to where worker injury is so rare as to be an uncommon event.

Chapter 4 - The Zero Injury Research- Summary

<u>*Origin of Zero Injury in the Construction Industry*</u>
It was in the late 1980's that the rare safety performance of "Zero Lost Workday Cases" came to the attention of a group of construction industry leaders.

This attention was brought to bear by Ed Donnelly, CEO of Air Products and Chemicals of Allentown, PA. Mr. Donnelly, seeing the results of their own safety management efforts directed at their contractors virtually eliminating serious injury, had a vision that such performance was within the reach of all. Mr. Donnelly then led his CEO peers, all members of the prestigious Business Roundtable, to begin recognizing contractors and owners for safety excellence. It was after Air Products was awarded the coveted Business Roundtable (BRT) Construction Industry Safety Excellence (CISE) award that Air Product's remarkable safety record in construction became public knowledge.

What was so remarkable? Listen to this. Air Products and Chemicals contracted 2,400,000 total work-hours of construction during 1984, 1985, 1986 and 1987. This was done using over 450 individual contractors across the USA in over 180 projects with a worker injury result of <u>Zero</u> OSHA Lost Workday Cases! And with a Recordable rate of only 2.1, which was some six to seven times better than the OSHA national average in those years.

Comparing Air Products performance to the industry average for those years, we see their approach to contractor safety management avoided some 130 lost workday cases and another 140+ Recordable cases. The question from Air Product's manufacturer owner peers, using the same construction industry resources, was simply put: "How do you do that?"

Another example was found in Winway, Inc., an industrial contractor located in Freeport, Texas, who was also honored with a BRT CISE award during 1988 for having achieved four years with their 600 employees without a lost workday case. This was for a total of 4,800,000 work-hours. Even more remarkable! Again the question arose: "How do you do that?"

Research Conducted

Dr. Richard Tucker, Director of the Construction Industry Institute (CII), Austin, Texas agreed to provided the answer to this critical question. The CII commissioned The Zero Accidents Task Force in late 1989. Dr. Roger Liska, of Clemson University, the Academician serving on the task force, performed the actual research in cooperation with the Task Force. The research project required nearly four years of effort by the task force members. The author served as Task Force Chairman.

This Task Force Mission was aimed at determining how some employers were able to work these millions of hours without serious injury to their employees while others found it difficult to have less than the then six ("the national average") lost workday cases per 200,000 hours worked. They studied 25 projects, eight of which were experiencing zero lost workday cases.

The August, 1993 Task Force report concluded that there were five critical safety techniques being used by these contractors who were successful in eliminating Lost Workday Cases. These were:
- Pre-project/Pre-task safety planning
- Safety orientation and Training
- Written safety incentive program
- Alcohol and substance abuse programs
- Accident/Incident investigations

More details of the 1993 research report are given in Chapter 9.

Industry Performance Results from the 1993 Research
In the years following many owners and contractors applied these techniques with gratifying success. Serious injury rates plummeted, schedules were improved and costs reduced.

During the years between 1993 and 2000 many contractors began experiencing "Zero Recordable" results on some projects. Thus it seemed that if the Zero Injury techniques were applied with certain other key safety management ingredients, it was possible to complete projects with Zero Recordable injuries.

When the initial research was completed in 1993 and published, the members of CII began using the Zero Injury techniques. The performance results of the CII member companies, when measured by OSHA/BLS Recordable rate, dropped from 7.20 in 1989 to 1.02 in 2001.

With these successes and the time lapse since the 1993 research report it seemed mandatory that follow-up research be accomplished. Thus in 1999 CII once again commissioned a research task force.

Follow-up Research Conducted
Ten years after CII commissioned "The Zero Accidents Task Force" a new task force was commissioned titled "Making Zero Accidents a Reality." CII reported the research results in August 2001 and August 2002.

This task force enlarged the number of critical safety management techniques to nine. These were:

The Zero Injury Guide Book

- Demonstrated management commitment
- Staffing for safety
- Safety planning
- Safety training and education
- Worker participation and involvement
- Recognition and rewards
- Subcontractor management
- Accident/incident reporting and investigations
- Drug and alcohol testing

The 1993 Research results are underlined. More details of the 2001/2002 research reports are given in Chapter 10.

The Questions

Will the principles found in the CII research apply to a workplace that is not in construction?

The answer is a clear "yes" with appropriate minor modifications.

The second question on the mind of those who do not walk the "Zero Injury high ground" is simply this:

"How do they do that?" Translated –

"If I can find out how they do that then perhaps we can also!"

If you are one of these people asking this question and are sincere in this interest, and wish to spend a few hours boning up on this topic, then you will find that there is "a recipe."

The process described in pages following can change your working culture and is applicable to any work place, be it transportation, manufacturing, mining, or simply an office staff. The process is universally applicable.

The third question on the mind of the interested is: "How do we get started?"

Well, if you have read this far, perhaps you already have started. It's up to you.

The fourth question is: "What is involved, what do we have to do?"

This book is your introduction and guide to implementing the Zero Injury concept. This process could be named "Creating a Zero Injury Working Culture." Read the guidebook. Apply what you read. As you go determine who the successful companies are and learn from them.

Chapter 5 – Corporate Leadership is Required

The CEO is Key

<u>Corporate Commitment</u>
The key research findings was: *In the zero lost workday injury companies the CEO always had a key operating safety expectation placed before the company management.* It was, paraphrased as follows -

"We will do our work without an injury. It is my (the CEO's) belief that all injury can be prevented and it is my expectation that there be no worker injury on our projects. And if an injury does occur it will not be viewed by me as acceptable performance! And I personally will be involved in determining how management failed. We will not set goals for injury! Our commitment is to ZERO Injury! This is not a statistics management effort. Rather our commitment shall be a complete devotion to the elimination of unsafe behavior by all employees, management and workers alike."

<u>A CEO Speaks</u>
I personally heard the CEO of a large construction company located on the West Coast tell of his experience regarding his attention to safety. He related that when he remained focused on safety he saw injury rates come down but if his attention was diverted for a time the injury rates rose.

Conclusion? CEO attention is mandatory!

The CII research found that in companies such as the examples listed above that, indeed over time, a successful "unsafe behavior will be avoided" culture had been established and was pervasive throughout the organization, reaching effectively into the hourly ranks.

Some realists will want to ask, "What is the difference

between the above position of adopting a commitment to Zero Injury and a more "normal" approach of, over time, setting increasingly more stringent goals for injury frequency? Doesn't the latter approach work just as well?

They add, "It is not realistic to expect zero injury; after all, injuries are always going to happen."

The author is the first to admit that, given we are working with fallible humans, injuries will occur. But remember the statement given above on page 14, "The fact that injuries occur does not mean they must occur!"

Many employers have proven this statement to be true. These have simply learned to use proven approaches to managing safety, involving the employees in unique ways to the point where employees "buy-in" and injury becomes a very rare event.

A corporate commitment to the concept of "zero injuries" carries the heavy responsibility of not only "talking the safety talk" but also "walking the safety talk."

"Walking the safety talk" means doing whatever it takes to prevent the next injury!

For those who have had such a commitment and failed, they failed because they did not "know how" to create a working culture where worker injury is rare to non-existent.

Management actions "must" unequivocally parallel management's spoken word. For Zero Injury to become reality these management actions must include the safety training of the worker.

"Training" is the vital complementary element that yields progress toward Excellence. Safety training is of paramount importance.

Once management actions are in harmony with the "talk", and the training is done, injuries caused by the "uninformed worker" disappear. Injuries caused by the "careless act" begin to disappear.

Once the "zero injury" concept is believed and accepted by the employees, injuries caused by worker loyalty disappear. Yes, if a loyal worker does not have a clear message from management that "at risk" behavior is not acceptable then some will take chances in the interest of being good and loyal workers. In a Zero Injury culture such actions are not condoned.

It is true, many injuries do occur out of "chance taking." Chance taking arises when the worker goes that extra mile to shorten the time (taking a shortcut) to accomplish a task, or when the worker attempts to prevent or reduce the damage once an accident is in the process of occurring.

One of the significant safety gains that comes with the commitment of "zero injuries" is that the employees know that it is no longer O.K. to take chances that might result in injury out of loyalty to the employer.

Zero Injury as a Concept has Reached Critical Mass

Achieving excellence in safety performance through the Zero Injury concept is becoming more and more the accepted norm in owner and contractor companies in the USA. I predict that the Zero Injury Concept movement has reached critical mass and will continue until it becomes the safety culture in much of American Industry.

The zero injury concept has already reached the status of "the cultural norm" in several regions of the USA. Among these are the Texas Gulf Coast Region, because of the Petrochemical industry that have led in setting the expectation that zero injury was what was desired. The San Francisco and Los Angeles region due to the influence of companies such as Chevron, and Shell Oil and the East Coast region for those contractors that work for E.I. du Pont who have long been the industrial leader in eliminating injury from their workforce. As this is written we have the steel companies such as US Steel who are making great strides in leading contractors in the Zero Injury Concept. And there are signs that the electric power industry is beginning to capitalize on the savings coming from a zero injury workforce. In recent times a major effort was launched in Canada to publicize and encourage contractors to embrace the Zero Accidents notion.

Setting Expectations at Zero

There is no substitute for the concept of setting the ZERO safety performance expectation for your employees! It should be the ongoing plan of each employer that employees working for them, directly or through a subcontractor, will "know" that the expectation is for "zero" injuries.

How you begin is critical. In the beginning the Zero Injury expectation needs to be believable by your employees. To ensure believability many are first setting their injury commitment to Zero Lost Time Cases. Wait, you say, all the time you have been talking about zero injuries and now you are saying set the commitment for zero lost time injuries.

There are two reasons for this approach. The first, if your employees have never been exposed to the zero injury concept, they will typically "laugh in your face" if told the commitment is to zero injury. The credibility of the Zero Injury Concept must be established over time.

The second reason is the concern about the potential for hidden injuries. Especially in a work force that for the first time is given the expectation to work injury free. Some begin by recognizing zero lost time injuries; then after achieving this performance for extended periods, change to zero recordable injuries as the recognition norm.

Around the USA in the year 2002 there were many examples of construction work sites where millions of hours were worked with no resulting "lost time case" injuries. There are a growing number of projects that are completed with Zero Recordables. In achieving this level of performance, human suffering is largely eliminated and the cost savings are very significant.

More and more participants in the construction business, both owners and contractors, are coming to realize that "zero" lost time injuries is achievable. And they are taking that first step; telling their employees that "zero" is the expectation. As a CEO, letting the employees know of your "zero" injury expectation requires another sobering commitment; safety support at the job site through a well-planned and executed safety program.

The Competitive Edge

Even though an employer's overhead for Workers' Compensation Insurance is passed on to the user of product or service, those who maintain a near zero injury level of excellence in safety performance have a competitive edge on those less skilled in eliminating injury in the workplace. The lower costs and improved productivity arising from the improved safety performance of zero injury flow to more competitive bidding and increased profits.

Chapter 6 – Injury Rates and the Cost of Injury

The OSHA/BLS Injury Rates
It is a fact that over the past 10 years injury rates in American construction have decreased significantly. Would I say that this decrease is totally explainable by the advent of the Zero Injury Concept?

No, I would not make such a statement, for I believe this reduction has been a result of the increased cost of injury and many positive actions within the industry and government such as listed below in no particular order:
1. OSHA attention to the safety standards.
2. Broader attention by Labor Unions to safety issues.
3. The simple cost of injury as driven by Workers' Compensation insurance.
4. Recognition of the significant indirect cost of injury.
5. Attention by the Business Roundtable Construction Committee in recognizing safety excellence.
6. Broader attention by Contractor Associations to recognizing safety achievements by their members.
7. The results of the Construction Industry Institute research into the Indirect Costs of Injury.
8. The results of the Construction Industry Institute research into projects with Zero Accidents.
9. The advent of a number of Behavior Based Safety consultants who deal with the leading indicators or precursors to injury.
10. The attention paid by the Safety Associations and Councils such as the American Society of Safety Engineers and the National Safety Council.

As a result of the above partial list of contributors, injury to the American construction worker has steadily declined since 1988.

Importantly, as a consequence, contractors and owners have spent less money in medical costs and less on the even more debilitating indirect cost of worker injury.

The solid evidence is in! Injury rates as measured by OSHA/BLS tell the story.

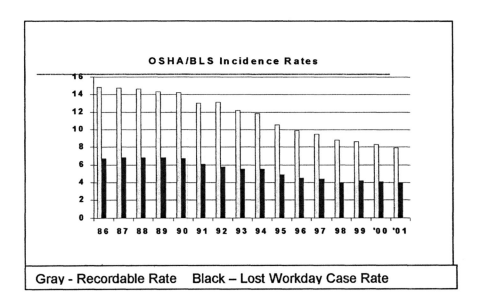

The above data do not extend beyond 2001 due to the lag in OSHA/BLS obtaining and processing the mass of data.

While this decrease is in itself gratifying, there is also an amazing reduction in injury rates by the member companies of the Construction Industry Institute (CII). These are the principal companies that have applied the Construction Industry Institute Zero Accident Task Force research results to their projects.

Note the 1993 research results have now been published nine years and most of the member companies have made significant improvements to the safety techniques revealed in the task force data. The following two charts comparing CII data to the OSHA/BLS data tell this amazing story.

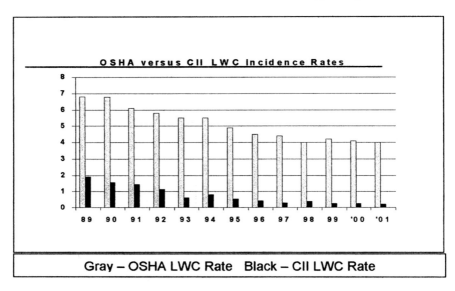

Gray – OSHA LWC Rate   Black – CII LWC Rate

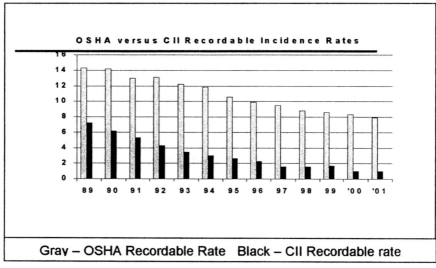

Gray – OSHA Recordable Rate   Black – CII Recordable rate

The CII data represent over 500,000,000 hours worked per year; thus, the impact on the national average is significant.

The Zero Injury Guide Book

OSHA Makes an Adjustment in 2002

Beginning in 2002 OSHA implemented new rules on how to make a judgement on if an injury is recordable or not. In short, the determination rules were tightened. This change will cause an increase in the averages for each employer and for industry averages in general. Whereas in the past each year OSHA required an annual report by each employer in the "OSHA 200 Log" format, the new form or format is named the "OSHA 300 Form or Log." Therefore, all historic records will not be exactly comparable to the current records. Of course, an employer could take the past records, alter them to bring all "record of injury" to the "OSHA 300 standard." Thus, comparisons can be made if desired.

The Cost of Injury

There are two ways to develop the total cost of injury. One is by using the actual data; the other is to analyze the underlying costs of carrying Worker's Compensation Insurance.

The direct costs of injuries as driven by actual injury costs vary widely between contractors because of the difference in how cases are managed. Some contractors make no attempt to get the injured back to work in a productive and medically approved work activity. In such cases the costs can get very high indeed.

However, the average costs of an injury, where the employer works actively with the medical provider to get a restricted work release, are much reduced. An employee back at work and productively engaged in activity that does not jeopardize his/her physical condition is known to heal more rapidly and thus is back on full duty sooner.

One thing I have noticed over the years is that as those contractors successfully utilizing the CII Zero Injury safety

The Zero Injury Guide Book

techniques watch injury rates fall each year, they also observe that the severity of the injuries that do occur is also much less. With reduced severity there is the obvious reduced cost.

Determining the average cost of injury as driven by Workers' Compensation Insurance premium can give one a notional look at injury cost that can be used to motivate top management to pay increased attention to safety.

Calculating the Average Cost of an Injury

In a broad sense this method takes the total cost of Workers' Compensation Insurance and divides by the number of injuries for the same period.

To get this cost we need to calculate the average premium for a construction situation. The premium is generally calculated by the following formula: (simplified)

Premium = Payroll x Manual Rate x EMR

Your immediate question may be, "What is EMR."

The short answer is, it is the ratio between your actual injury losses to your expected losses. The higher your losses due to injury the higher the EMR and a high EMR is a costly thing to have to endure. I have heard of EMR in the range of 3.00 and I have heard of EMR in the range of 0.20. Obviously the one you want is the lower one.

Your next question may be, "What is Manual Rate?"

The Manual Rate is the Workers' Compensation Insurance rate per $100 of payroll. These rates are different by trade and by state. If two rates are the same in two different states it will be a coincidence. These rates in construction range from $3 or $4 dollars to as high as near $100 in the more injury prone trades in some states.

Using 100 workers let's assume the EMR is 1.00 and the payroll is $4,000,000. This payroll would represent 100 workers at a $20.00 wage rate for one year. This wage is applied to 2000 work-hours per employee per year.

The serious injury (OSHA lost workday case) rate per 100 workers was 4.0 in the year 2001. Experience has shown that about 95% of all injury costs are attributable to Lost Workday Cases.

The national average "16 trade" Workers' Compensation "Manual Rate" for construction in the USA is about $13.00 per $100 payroll.

Thus: Nominal Premium = (4,000,000 x 13/100 x 1.00 = $520,000 for 100 workers.

The OSHA/BLS total recordable rate for the year 2001 was 7.90. By subtracting the 4.0 from 7.9 we get 3.9 other Recordables (7.9 – 4.0 = 3.9). If we estimate the cost of each non-lost time recordable at $1,500 and multiply by 3.9 we get $5,850. Then by subtracting $5,850 from the $520,000 we get $514,150 as the cost of the 4.0 Lost Workday cases. If we then divide $514,150 by "four point zero" (4.0) we get $128,537 premium per each lost workday case.

Remember this $128,537 is only the national average premium cost paid per lost workday case. Also recognize the above calculation does not consider other cost factors that may be included in a Workers' Comp. policy, such as insurance carrier discounts, etc., which reduce overall premium for the affected contractors. Such factors may lessen the cost for these.

So right away one can see the desirability of an EMR around 0.20 (the best I have seen). With a 0.20 EMR the total premium for such a contractor falls from $520,000 to $104,000 per 100 workers. Conversely the premium rises for an EMR of 3.00 to $1,560,000, a $1,456,000 difference. By the way, this saving does not include the reduced indirect cost that is at least double the premium just calculated.

Calculating the Total Cost of an Injury
To get the total cost, the average cost must be adjusted to include the average indirect cost of an injury. CII research conducted in 1988 found that the indirect costs of the average injury are 2 to 20 times the direct costs (medical and indemnity). But for the sake of a conservative approach, lets assume only a "one to one ratio."

To find a pure indirect cost out of the Workers' Compensation premium we need to reduce the per injury premium above by the amount of insurance carrier overhead and profit then add the remaining amount. See example calculation following.

Let's say that carrier's charge an average of about 30% for overhead and profit. This reduces the $125,292 by 30% or $37,587 leaving the estimated pure indirect costs at $87,705. Adding this to the premium charge brings the total cost of a single lost workday case to $212,997.

Explaining the Cost Result
If this $212,997 looks high, it is. It is high for many in 2001 because in a number of states the manual rates are higher than they need be so the carriers will give deep discounts on premiums. Notice, I said in a number of states. Counter balancing this, some states have such a lenient Workers' Compensation administrative process that it results in significant misuse and fraud, which has become all too

common. In those states this dramatically drives up the costs to the employer.

Also the costs look high because for many contractors the total of $212,997 is what I term the cost of negligence. This could be the cost where a contractor paid no attention to their Workers' Compensation coverage or to getting the injured back to work. In such cases, then, these higher numbers may well represent the true cost. In any case such a number is sobering to see!

With a successful Zero Injury initiative in place and functioning well, coupled with an alert case management process utilizing the latitudes allowed to insure return to work when appropriate, these costs are much lower. It is the experience of the CII companies that the average cost of a lost workday case injury will run around $50,000 including indirect costs. Of course this lower cost also varies from contractor to contractor and will also vary from region to region as medical costs, wages, and state partial wage vary.

Again, please note that, the estimated $212,997 is the national average cost, as mentioned above, of doing no case management; in which case, I term the above figure the cost of negligence. Sadly there are some who fall in this category.

Chapter 7 - Zero Injury Return on Investment

The Basics
Would Zero Injury be of more interest if I told you that it is routine for successful users to get a 200-300% ROI on the cost of implementation and evergreen safety program maintenance?

There are a number of questions regarding data gathering surrounding the effort to calculate the ROI obtainable when changing a safety culture from "injuries happen" to one that embraces the Zero Injury Concept (and ultimately achieves Zero injury on a scale with world class performance.)

In today's age we all know the costs of injury are very high. But little do we realize that it is a lot higher than we think. The "direct cost of injury" (that covered by Workers' Compensation) is given to us in our Workers' Compensation management processes when we audit our "Loss Run." By adding to our "injury losses" our hidden "losses in efficiency," then calculating an ROI on the expense required to reduce the cost of injury, one can see that the undeniable result is "pure gold" to the bottom line.

The "losses in efficiency" derived from employee injury are calculated by using the CII research derived ratios between Injury Losses and "losses in efficiency, termed indirect costs." This research performed by CII in 1988, gave the industry hard numbers on the indirect cost of injury. Yet employers are seldom, if ever, using these data to generate enthusiasm for Zero Injury as a workplace norm through an ROI calculation.

What if a company took their actual "direct cost" data and combined it with the CII research based Ratio between Direct and Indirect cost, and then combined this information in a calculation to determine ROI for the added money spent while in the process of embracing the Zero Injury Process? My experience reveals that the "pay-out" from reduced injury on successfully applying the Zero Injury principles is not a paltry 10-25% but an amazing 200-300%. I ask the reader; "Is there a quicker way to increase profit than this?"

Company leaders work endless hours to develop business, and then more hours preparing and performing the work, all more often than not, for a slim and optimistic 5 to 10% profit margin. They do this, while right in the midst of the management process, is an opportunity to get returns on investment of 300%! Since we are talking employee safety, of course, this opportunity rests in how safety in managed.

If you are one of those that are managing safety the same way year after year, with near average unsatisfactory results, then you are the one that will gain the highest from your ROI on spending the money to install a Zero Injury Safety Culture in your company.

This author applied such specific data (real data) and the ROI result is astounding! Would you believe a 300% return is normal? This is not just in the first year of the calculation. Once near Zero Injury is achieved the 300% will be there annually as long as the application of the Zero Injury concept yields world class injury statistics, year after year after year.

Learning this should be an "eye-catching" revelation to company leaders and a wake up call to drive safety success to world class. The Zero Injury effort is most rewarding for those who enjoy performance that are near or over the OSHA/BLS national averages. The closer you are to Zero Injury when you start, the less the ROI on Zero Injury calculation effort will yield. But even if you are down in the 100% ROI range, it cannot be considered as anything other than a "brilliant investment of time and energy."

What is World Class Performance
We touched on this in Chapter 2. World-class performance is working with no injury: Zero OSHA Recordables. There are many companies that achieve zero injury every year. Some have done so with millions of hours worked. It is now common for large and some small companies to accumulate runs of 1,000,000 work-hours with no (Zero) OSHA Recordables injuries. This is world class. You will be world class when you do the same. And you can.

For industries where lost time injury OSHA frequency rates are high, above 2.00 up to 6.00, the pay out is largest. If you have one lost time injury each year and it costs $100,000 and you spend $50,000 to eliminate that injury you are getting a return of 200%. Getting these numbers, in exact terms, is the reason most do not attempt to do an ROI calculation. But in all reality these numbers can be obtained quite easily.

Do not allow fear of complexity to become an excuse for not applying your own numbers and discovering the greatest of all possible discoveries: Not aggressively protecting your employee asset is tantamount to management delinquency!

Are you ready to begin?

Start by Selecting a Base Year
ROI must be calculated from a financial base. In this case the base is the year before you begin applying the zero injury techniques, or from where you are now. Perhaps you are sparing nothing and putting your all into having a superior safety team and program yet the results are not there. You are somewhat better than the national average in your

your industry but not by very much. At least it is not a performance that brings you satisfaction.

The above position is where I was, for far too many years, so I can relate to it; working hard at achieving good results, but not seeing the progress I longed to see. I was still seeing way too many serious injuries. So this is the type of "here and now" that becomes your base year in the ROI calculation.

Off your base year, you go to work to learn all the aspects of implementing a Zero Injury safety initiative modeled around the CII research results. You get the information and lay out your plan. You will likely need more safety staff to accomplish all of the activities that the CII research indicates is needed. You will likely need to spend more time training your employees for safety, both in indoctrination of new employees and in pure safety training of all employees. Then there is the communication with your current employees. You will need to formally inform them of your newly found vision. This is likely the least expensive part.

It is, in the purest sense, a selling job you have to do. You have to sell your workers and supervision on your zero injury vision. You do this in "word – telling them of your vision" and in "deed - by changing the way safety has always been managed." Then you ask them for help. Help in learning and applying the proven CII zero injury techniques.

Crunching the Numbers

Lets' say you start this Zero Injury venture at the beginning of a new fiscal year. Your base year then becomes the year just past. Base year safety program costs are fixed as is, but future year's costs must be categorized into two parts.
1. The base year cost is the cost of the effort you now expend keeping your firm in compliance with OSHA standards and operating your safety program.

2. The cost of implementing the zero injury initiative that is going to drive your injuries down toward the zero mark. This number comes into play the first year of the zero injury effort.

Number 2 (two) is to be the pure costs of all the new Zero Injury initiative; the things you are going to do that you were not doing in the base year.

Do not transfer the nominal costs of how you have managed safety in the past into category two. Leave these in your current effort of compliance. You may be giving incentives and rewards for safety achievements. This area will need to be re-addressed, for in the future you will want to be doing your recognition and rewarding around the achievement measures that show proactive injury prevention activities.

The following information is explanatory for the Figures appearing in the Appendix under Item 4, page 193.

First in line of data gathering, we will need to capture base year numbers of injuries by category: total Recordables, and number of Lost Time Cases (LTC's). With these we will calculate the number of "pure" Recordable Cases (RC - those that were not LTC's.)

For example, say the Total number of Recordables was seven (7) with two (2) LTC's leaving five (5) of the Recordables as "pure." We need the numbers in this fashion for the most significant costs coming out of injury to employees is found in the LTC's.

Next, you will want to determine in some detail what your injury costs (losses) have been during your base year. These costs (losses) will be those that are categorized as base year costs in your ROI calculation. The numbers needed fall into

two categories, 1. Numbers of claims and 2. The estimated total developed cost of claims, as follows:
1. Total number of workers compensation claims filed in the base year.
2. Separate claims as one of the following:
   a. Claims that were classified as an OSHA Recordable injury. (RC)
   b. Claims that were classified as an OSHA Lost Time injury. (LTC)
   c. Pure recordables - calculate c. by subtracting b. from a. This becomes your number of claims arising from pure Recordables (non LTC's.)
   d. Number of claims that were not associated with being a pure Recordable or a LT injury.
3. Total Losses for the base year including current reserves and development allowances.
4. Then break your total losses down according to 2. a, b, c, and d. above.
5. Obtain averages for each claim type. Divide 2 b into 4 b, 2 c into 4 c, and 2 d into 4 d. for these averages.

Example – Say 2 b is 2 and 4 b is $200,000. By the above division we determine the average direct cost of a LTC is $100,000. Lets assume 2 c is 5 and 4 c is $2,500, we determine that the average cost of a Recordable loss is $500. Then lets assume 2 d is 2 and 4 d is $50,000 and we determine that the average cost of a non-OSHA claim is $25000. The averages will vary employer to employer.

6. Thus the cost of the average claim in each category is calculated. We need these numbers to do the financial forecasting for future years as you predict the improvement in safety performance (number of injuries) and improvement in claims management.

The Zero Injury Guide Book

Next identify all your Base year safety management costs by broad categories. Sum these as the total cost of running your traditional approach to safety program. The expenditures you incur for implementing your zero injury initiative are to be kept separately so the ROI can be calculated as the number of injuries become less.

Indirect cost avoidance in a significant part of the savings you are going to enjoy and these are much higher than most people realize. Therefore, next we are going to apply the research results of CII to calculate the indirect costs of injury to round out your base year losses. Multiply your direct losses due to LWC's by 2.08 and your direct losses due to pure Recordables by 1.16. (In the judgment of some these multipliers are not large enough; in the mind of others they are too large. Know this; they were obtained by pure research into over 700 injuries by CII.) Add these figures to your total insured losses and this gives the total cost of injury for the base year. You will not calculate indirect costs for those claims that were not associated with an injury that was recordable.

Next we will sum the indirect costs and the direct cost of claims losses to arrive at the total costs for the base year.

By tracking reduced injury cost to offset any increased expense affiliated with the zero injury effort one can calculate an ROI on the cost of implementation and maintenance cost of your zero injury effort.

See Appendix Item 4, page 193 for a detailed explanation and table illustrating the ROI calculation.

Chapter 8 - Redefining Safety Commitment

The Question
All agree that, if an injury free workplace is to exist, management and worker COMMITMENT is a very essential and critical factor.

But what does the term "commitment" really mean when used to describe one's devotion to an injury free workplace? Has the term "commitment" become so all encompassing that it has no meaning? The term "committed" is often used in the following way:

> *"Though I was committed before, back then I thought that all injuries could not be prevented, but I have changed. Now I am really committed. Not just a little, I mean a huge increase in my commitment."*

It is commonly true and reasonable to state that all the people involved in a work process are "committed" to the thesis that "no one will want" injury to occur. But is this "no one will want" feeling everyone has, the only essential ingredient in defining "commitment?"

On examination, the broad range of meaning in which we find the word "commitment" used leads to an unsatisfactory answer. Immediately, it is apparent that to define "commitment" we must go far beyond superficial definitions.

The pivotal question then is: Are we, the management, and the employees COMMITTED, "in fact," to a safe workplace, when we find that in the year 2001 the OSHA/BLS national average for injury in construction was still as many as 7.9 Recordables per 100 workers per year? Manufacturing is even worse at 8.1 Recordables, with all of private industry at 5.7. Are we, "in fact," COMMITTED when we set goals that recognize (thus allow) a certain number of injuries per year?

The Zero Injury Guide Book

Embedded in the Zero Injury thesis is this fact:

==We are not committed to an injury free workplace until we embrace the notion that all injury is preventable, that no injury is acceptable and that we will not sacrifice schedule, cost or production over an injury free workplace. Nor will we set injury goals, thereby inadvertently indicating that some number of injuries is expected and hence acceptable.==

In recent years when asked to define safety commitment, most people would agree to the answer, "Safety commitment is in evidence when the workplace is free of unsafe behavior." Where work places with very low unsafe behaviors are found, it is also found that management and employees alike are sold on a unique safety management process.

How does one create such a workplace?

What are the key management ingredients?

What are the crucial safety management techniques?

"Commitment" Definitions Explored

What do we generally mean when we say "I am committed to this safety program?"

Or what do we mean when we as managers say, "I am 'committed' to preventing injury for humanitarian reasons to the best of my ability?"

In our social life the word "committed" implies a certain level of devotion to a person, principle or an activity such as a job.

Defined by Webster, "commitment" means; "To bind as by a promise or pledge."

But, as we all know, the practical result in defining anyone's active "commitment" to a theme or thesis, will result in a broad range of action from little, if any, to a lot.

In our daily conversations we admit, inadvertently, that the word "commitment" is not a well defined in any exact sense thus is an inaccurately understood word. Often when we use the word "commitment," we further define our meaning by adding definitive words such as "totally committed" or "really committed" or "completely committed." Or we may even say, "I am a lot more committed now than I was then." These definitive and qualifying words are used because we subconsciously recognize there are varying levels or degrees of "commitment."

What one person describes as "commitment" can be far greater or significantly less than that of a colleague when measured in resulting energy or effective management effort.

We even have analogies we use to define our meaning of commitment. One of these is "Commitment means that we would lay down our life to prevent the loss of another's life." This is likely the outer extreme of all the "commitment" definitions and is sometimes found to be present in very close relationships.

The weakest definition for being committed to safety in the workplace would be to simply say, "I am committed," but in fact take no action whatsoever to prevent an injury to another or to even be a good example.

Since defining "commitment" is so difficult, should we then avoid all use of the word in relation to safety performance? Or should we who are concerned about safety management seek a new definition that makes the word "commitment" more usable in the field of safety management?

The Zero Injury Definition of Commitment

There is a growing recognition emerging from the practice of safety management that the meaning of the word "commitment" is demonstrated in its most meaningful definition when a person or firm takes the philosophical position that - "no injury is acceptable. All injuries are preventable and we will do whatever it takes to prevent injury." The position "injury is unacceptable" puts all employees, the CEO, management and employees, of a company on the same footing. Such a definition is commonly found among those who embrace the safety philosophy now commonly known as the *"Zero Injury Concept"*

The "Zero Injury Concept" is not a safety management theory that a few safety professionals, academics and graduate students invented. Rather, the "Zero Injury Concept" is what a small number of companies (owners and contractors) in the construction industry, largely unknown to each other, perfected a decade ago as the normal performance result of their individual safety programs.

Most people in industry will agree that, for the very best in safety performance to occur, management must somehow provide a cultural platform in the company where everyone focuses attention on a continuing basis to working safe. The attention is devoted to seeking that long period of time when no injuries occur.

The Zero Injury Commitment and Profit Margin

At this point, the key question of cost effectiveness is raised when we use the term "profit margin." After all, "profit margin," management enthusiasts say, is what we are in business to achieve. This is a basic truth, so the "alleged" proposition of pursuing safety at the expense of profit has a few tough decision points built in.

The Zero Injury Guide Book

Are the people so concerned about the cost correct? In part they are. We (management and safety professionals) would sometimes like to argue that all safety effort is driven by humanitarian reasons. But we also know that staying in business also requires good stewardship of the profit margin. In dealing with this vital point the zero injury practitioners reveal a startling discovery about the cost, time and effort required to include all the proven zero injury techniques in a safety program.

When the zero injury practitioners applied all the necessary energy into all the planning and coordination to insure an injury free workplace they found that these were the same planning activities they must use to get the job done effectively anyway. In short, the zero injury companies find that zero injury planning actually results in a more profitable project because their "no injury is acceptable" safety commitment becomes the catalyst that forces a more detailed planning process. The worker's time is used more efficiently and, more importantly, employees' attitudes toward the work are more supportive since they are involved in insuring that safe work plans are being made and followed.

This is especially true at the supervisor/foreman/worker interface. It is commonplace for supervisors/foremen to push production and, as a result, often give inadequate time to detailed planning of the day's activities. The project suffers in productivity, and injuries occur as well, when insufficient planning is being done.

The Zero Injury technique of "Pre-task Safety Planning" forces the foremen and employees to give sufficient time to planning in the name of safety to insure a safe installation (safe production) process. This, in turn, yields an improved execution of the plan that, in turn, improves productivity then improved profit.

One foreman said to me during an interview, "I have never involved my crew in making work plans, I just tell them what to do and expect them to do it." Any thoughtful manager knows that, when the entire crew is involved in making an execution plan, the productivity will be much improved.

Commitment Redefined Increases Profits
Commitment redefined, in the Zero Injury Concept, has uncovered the (not so astonishing) relationship between worker safety and profitability. This phenomenon of "profit in safety" is easily understood when one considers the reduced numbers of costly injuries, the reduced indirect costs that go with injuries, the enhanced worker buy-in to the safety process, and the detailed safety planning, all resulting in more efficiently executed work.

> One could say that you can plan to do the work and leave safety considerations out, but one cannot do the planning to work safely and not plan the work!

"Safety and planning," a powerful combination resulting in improved results if our priorities are right.

The Conclusion
Defining COMMITMENT as the CEO's pledge to an injury free workplace solves the production (schedule, cost, and profit) versus safety dilemma.

The CEO's pledge that worker injury is unacceptable for humanitarian reasons answers the question of how we in the safety professions should define the word COMMITMENT. Current testimony coming from CEO's, embracing the Zero Injury notion that injury is unacceptable, tells the world that commitment to Zero Injury by your employees is not only achievable but is essential for a company to be at the top of its' business and profit potential.

Chapter 9 - The 1993 Construction Industry Institute Zero Accident/Injury Research In Detail

The 1993 Research

The Construction Industry Institute (CII) affiliated with The University of Texas at Austin, took on a research effort in 1989 looking into the occurrence of "Zero" Lost Workday Cases on construction projects. In 1987, it became public knowledge that some contractors in construction work, the most dangerous of all industries in the year 1987, were working millions of hours without OSHA Lost Workday Cases. Industry leaders asked the obvious question.

"How do they do that?"

Leaders in The Construction Industry Institute volunteered to undertake a research project to determine the answer. The Zero Accident Task Force was formed in 1989 and finished in 1993. Emmitt J. Nelson retired Shell Oil Company Construction Relations Manager served as Chairman. A total of 16 members including Dr. Roger Liska of Clemson University made up the group. The purpose of The Zero Accidents Task Force was:

1) To show owners and contractors how to achieve zero accidents on construction projects.
2) To convince management of the value of an effective safety program, through research, by identifying techniques most successful in achieving zero accidents.

The research was conducted through interviews at 25 construction projects. Seventeen of these projects had an average Lost Workday Case Incident Rate of 0.25. Another eight projects had an average Lost Workday Case Incidence Rate of 2.5, ten times worse.

In order to obtain viable research information three data sets were obtained.

The first data set was the result of interviewing over 400 hundred Trades people by asking each to name the three most important safety techniques being used.

The second data set was the result of asking Trades people and leaders alike for the amount of time being spent on 17 critical safety techniques. The following two questions are examples.

"How much time do you spend in safety meetings?"

"How much time do you spend in Pre-Task Safety Planning?"

The third data set resulted from determining which of a list of 170 commonly known safety techniques were being used by each project.

Out of these data the final research findings were assembled.

The 1993 Findings

After nearly four years of work the task force reported, in late 1993, the top five principal safety techniques with important sub-techniques being used by those contractors achieving Zero Lost Workday Case Injury:

1. Safety Pre-Project/Pre-Task Planning
    a. Pre-Project planning
        i. Safety goals (not injury goals)
        ii. Safety person/personnel
        iii. Pre-placement employee physical evaluation

    b. Pre-Task planning
        i. Task Hazard analysis
        ii. Task training

2. Safety Orientation and Training
   a. Site orientation
   b. Owner involved in orientation
   c. Safety policies and procedures covered
   d. Project specific orientation
   e. Formal safety training

3. Written safety incentive program
   a. Cents per hour for the workers
   b. Spot cash incentives used with workers
   c. Milestone cash incentives given to workers
   d. End of project incentives given to workers

4. Alcohol and Substance Abuse Program (ASAP)
   a. Pre-employment Screening done for alcohol and drugs
   b. Screening conducted at random
   c. Inspections for contraband conducted
   d. Post accident screening done for all employees
   e. All project contractors have ASAP's

5. Accidents/Incidents Investigations
   a. Near hit Incidents investigated
   b. Near hits are reported to home office
   c. Accidents without injury investigated
   d. Project accident review team established for all accidents or incidents
   e. Project work exposure hours and safety statistics reported to home office

Techniques - Time Quantity Versus Quality
The research data show that quantity of time spent on selected techniques is not as important as the quality of time spent. An even more significant point is this; in an evolving safety program the selection of the specific safety technique to spend time on becomes more crucial than how much overall time is spent on it.

As an example, time spent in pre-project/pre-task planning

results in earlier hazard identification and more hazard control and elimination, therefore, the project will require less hazard discussion and protection. This would result in less time spent on other techniques, such as safety meetings and accident investigation.

Of paramount importance was to, somehow, obtain the buy-in of the Trades people. It was found that, unless they are convinced that management was indeed serious about achieving a zero injury result, the actual result was less than satisfactory.

1993 Research Task Force Conclusions
The task force research provided the following conclusions regarding achieving zero injuries.

* Zero Lost Workday Cases was being achieved on all types of construction and maintenance projects.

* Zero Lost Workday Cases was being achieved by contractors, small and large, and on many projects, even large projects with several million work-hours.

* Zero Lost Workday Cases was being achieved in all project labor situations: i.e., union, merit or non-union.

* Joint owner and contractor senior management devotion to "ZERO" is key in achieving this level of performance. Setting this expectation for project workers at all levels is a vital first step.

* The presence of an effective safety program producing "good" safety performance must contain a broad base of essential safety techniques similar to those contained in the 170-technique list. See CII Publication 32.1 "Zero Injury Techniques."

The Zero Injury Guide Book

* Attaining zero injuries is significantly more likely on Projects that apply the Five High Impact Zero Injury Techniques that were identified.

* Success in eliminating accidents is not guaranteed by use of the Five High Impact Zero Injury Techniques alone.

* Quality of effort is strongly suggested by the "Time Spent" data as a vital ingredient in reaching zero injury.

1993 Research Group Recommendations
The task force offers the following recommendations:

* Adopt the "Zero Injury" philosophy, beginning with the chief executive officer (CEO) who sets the expectation that worker injury is unacceptable on all work.

* Create a culture where all employees, at all levels, accept ownership of the safety performance objective of "Zero Injuries." The CEO sets the expectation and empowers all employees to do what is necessary to reach zero injury performance.

* Recognize that profit lost through worker injury is not covered by insurance.

* Institutionalize a comprehensive basic safety process using the 170 safety techniques identified by the research.

* Establish specific contract requirements defining the roles and responsibilities of all parties (companies) involved in reaching zero injury.

* Define, explicitly, the safety responsibilities and authorities for all project personnel (leaders and workers) involved in the project.

* Implement The Five High Impact Zero Injury Safety Techniques.

* Recognize quality of effort is more important than time spent, as techniques are implemented.

* Understand that the high cost of Workers' Compensation is driven by worker injury and that achieving zero injury performance is a key component of responsible management for profit.

* Conduct a safety assessment.

* The owner should be an active participant as the project embraces the "Zero Injury" philosophy.

* Insure that subcontractors are active participants.

The Application of 1993 Research Data Leads to Zero Recordable Performance

Even as the 1993 research was being conducted it was apparent that safety performance in the construction industry was experiencing a step change of improvement. After the research results were reported, numerous CII member companies began implementation of the Zero Injury principles.

Soon these owners and contractors were requiring use of the Zero Injury techniques by all those working on their projects. As this cadre of contractors and owners enlarged, the movement toward adopting the Zero Injury Concept gathered momentum. It was at this stage that the technique of involving all employees in the Zero Injury process found broad support. It became immediately apparent that employee involvement took the frequency of injuries to a new lower level; Zero Recordables. This was apparent, because many contractors began experiencing Zero Recordable injuries for longer and longer periods of time.

By 1997 many in the construction industry saw that follow-up research was going to be necessary in order to firmly establish the extended family of Zero Injury Techniques that were producing these Zero Recordable results. Thus in 1999, CII launched the next research effort, "Making Zero Accidents a Reality." The 1999 beginning resulted in new results in 2001.

Chapter 10 - The 2001/2002 Construction Industry Institute Zero Accident/Injury Research In Detail

From Zero Lost Workday to Zero Recordable Cases

Construction industry safety performance progress was solidly verified when the researchers noted that among the 38 projects there were four that were working at the Zero Recordable level when the research was conducted.

Though in 1993 the recordable incident rate on only one project was below 1.00, the Zero Recordable performance was not being achieved with sufficient regularity and length of time to notice. The best in the 1993 research project group of 25 had a Recordable Incident rate of 0.87, which was excellent for the time.

The 2001 Research

Almost exactly a decade after the original Construction Industry Institute (CII) research began in 1989 (results released in 1993), CII once again, in 1999, commissioned a task force to examine recent successes in working injury free in construction. These results were released in 2001

This time, however, the task force would examine the frequent occurrence of "Zero Recordable Injuries" on construction projects. The "Making Zero Accidents a Reality Task Force" was formed with John Mathis of Bechtel as Chairman. A total of 14 members including Dr. Jimmie W. Hinze of the University of Florida made up the group. The purpose, as issued by CII leaders, was:

- Make zero accidents a reality through research and identification of current Zero Accident best practices that have proven results across a broad spectrum of the construction industry.

This mission was later expanded as follows:
- Develop a communication and education component to assist in understanding and implementation of best practices that support a Zero Accidents culture.

The task force conducted two separate studies:
- Large construction firms and
- Large construction projects

Questionnaires were sent to the Engineering News Record 400 largest contractors. There were 102 responses. Detailed interviews were conducted on 38 North American construction projects ranging in size from $50 million to $600 million. The 38 projects covered the following six types of construction:
Petrochemical – Industrial - Public Works
Transportation - Hotel - Commercial buildings

The 2001 Findings

As given above the task force found there were nine "Best Practices" that were critical underpinnings of a Zero Injury culture.
These were:
- Demonstrated management commitment
- Staffing for safety
- <u>Safety planning</u>
- <u>Safety training and education</u>
- Worker participation and involvement
- <u>Recognition and rewards</u>
- Subcontractor management
- <u>Accident/incident reporting and investigations</u>
- <u>Drug and alcohol testing</u>

Those underlined were the five 1993 research results. Clearly the 2001 research clarified the need for appropriate numbers of safety personnel, and the absolute necessity of management to demonstrate their commitment. Emphasized by the 2001 results were the extremely important message of employee involvement. It is clear that ways to obtain employee "buy-in" and support is absolutely essential. Pay attention to sub-contractor management, insuring that all contractors on the project are combining their collective skills in the avoidance of unsafe conditions and unsafe behavior.

~~It is when all workers see this total and coordinated commitment that they actually begin to believe that their employers are really serious about this subject called "safety."~~ With this belief, the advent of injury free work finds its fruition.

CULTURE

Technique Relative Impact

A number of specific sub-techniques were examined seeking to determine the impact each technique had on the reduction of Recordable Injuries. In each case the Task force compared those projects using the technique against those who were not using the technique and reported the average Recordable Rate for each class.

<u>Demonstrated Management Commitment:</u>
Top management participates in investigation of Recordable injuries.
- Participates in every injury – RIR = 1.20
- Participates in 50% or less – RIR = 6.89

Company President/senior management reviews safety performance record.
- Yes – RIR = 0.97
- No – RIR = 6.89

Frequency of home office safety inspections on the project.
- Weekly/Bi-weekly – RIR = 1.33
- Monthly/Annually – RIR = 2.63

<u>Safety Staffing</u>
Number of workers per safety professional – see explanation
- 50 or less – RIR = 1.33
- Over 50 – RIR = 2.35

To whom does safety representative report?
- Corporate Staff – RIR = 1.38
- Project Line – RIR = 2.41

The Zero Injury Guide Book

Safety Planning
  Does the project have a site-specific safety program?
  - Yes – RIR = 1.76
  - No – RIR = 5.43

  Are Pre-task meetings held?
  - Yes – RIR = 1.04
  - No – RIR = 2.67

Safety Training and Education
  Is safety training a line item within the budget?
  - Yes – RIR = 1.38
  - No – RIR = 2.63

  Does every worker on-site receive a safety orientation?
  - Yes – RIR = 1.76
  - No – RIR = 5.72

  Is format of safety orientation formal as opposed to informal?
  - Yes – RIR = 1.51
  - No – RIR = 3.80

  Do workers receive at least 4 hours per month of safety training after orientation?
  - Yes – RIR = 0.94
  - No – RIR = 2.79

  Do superintendents and project managers receive at least 4 hours safety training per month?
  - Yes – RIR = 1.07
  - No - RIR = 2.00

  When are tailgate meetings held?
  - On Mondays – RIR = 3.25
  - On Tuesdays/Wednesdays/Thursdays – RIR = 2.00
  - Daily – RIR = 1.00 (When Pre-task safety planning is used.)

Worker Involvement and Participation
  Are safety perception surveys conducted on the project?
  - Yes – RIR = 1.33
  - No – RIR = 2.82

  Do management and supervisory personnel receive behavior overview training?
  - Yes – RIR = 1.38
  - No – RIR = 2.82

The Zero Injury Guide Book

Does a formal worker-to-worker behavior observation program exist on the project?
- Yes – RIR = 1.38
- No – RIR = 2.82

Does the total number of safety observation reports filed on the project exceed 100?
- Yes – RIR = 1.01
- No – RIR = 1.93

Recognition and Rewards
Does the project have a formal worker incentive program?
- Yes – RIR = 3.20*
- No – RIR = 2.05
  * This incentive was one of a single large prize at the end of the project.

Is recognition incentive based on zero injury objectives?
- Yes – RIR = 1.33
- No – RIR = 3.29

How often are recognition incentives given to workers?
- Weekly/bi-weekly – RIR = 1.33
- Quarterly – RIR = 3.29

Do family members attend safety dinners?
- Yes – RIR = 0.18
- No – RIR = 2.35

Are field supervisors evaluated on safety?
- Yes – RIR =2.00
- No – RIR = 8.89

Subcontractor management
Are subcontractors required to submit site-specific safety plans?
- Yes – RIR = 1.37
- No – RIR = 3.83

Do all subcontractor workers attend a formal standard safety orientation?
- Yes – RIR = 3.30
- No – RIR = 5.33

How frequently do subcontractors hold safety meetings/pre-task?
- Daily – RIR = 1.04
- Weekly – RIR = 2.45

The Zero Injury Guide Book

Are there sanctions for subcontractor non-compliance with safety standards?
- Yes – RIR = 1.43
- No – RIR = 5.35

Accident/Incident Reporting and Investigation
Number of near hits recorded on the project?
- Over 50 reported – RIR = 0.57
- Under 50 – RIR = 2.35

To what extent are recordable incidents investigated by top management?
- Every injury – RIR = 2.00
- 50% or less – RIR = 5.60

Results of Contractors implementing all nine Best Practices
- Jobs that implement most – RIR = 0.17
- Jobs that implement a few – RIR = 3.84

Evaluating Your Safety Culture

The CII "Making Zero Accidents a Reality" task force created a 24-point Safety Cultural Evaluation form. Opposite each of the 24 techniques you need only answer "yes" when you are effectively using the technique. Once completed you need only to give the completed list a quick glance to get a feel for how close you are to fulfilling the basic requirements for a climate where a Zero Injury Culture can exist.

The 24 techniques are: (order rearranged)
1. The president/senior company management reviews safety reports generated by the projects.
2. Top management has involvement in injury/ incident / accident investigations.
3. Management and supervision are evaluated on safety performance.
4. The project safety representatives report directly to company senior management.

5. The company maintains a minimum of one safety representative to 50 workers. (See appendix page 157 for clarification.)
6. The project has a site-specific safety plan.
7. Before each task, a task safety analysis / pre-task planning meeting is held with the foreman's crew.
8. Safety training is a line item in the project budget.
9. Every worker on the project attends a standard orientation training session.
10. The safety orientation training is formal.
11. Workers receive an average of at least four hours of safety training each month.
12. Superintendents and project managers attend mandatory safety training sessions.
13. All levels of management and supervision receive training in behavior based safety management.
14. A structured worker-to-worker safety observation program is maintained.
15. The company/project supports and maintains an effective near miss reporting process.
16. A formal documented system exists to report near misses.
17. Workers are encouraged to report near misses.
18. Safety recognition / rewards are given to the workers at least monthly.
19. Family members are included in safety recognition dinners.
20. Workers are evaluated on safety performance.
21. Subcontractors are required to submit project specific safety plans.
22. Sanctions are imposed when subcontractors do not comply with safety requirements.
23. Safety perception surveys (worker input) are conducted on the projects.
24. Off-site company personnel perform frequent audits/ assessments.

Worker Involvement and Participation Interventions

During the eight years between 1993 and 2001, a safety technique known as Behavior Based Safety (BBS) that involves the craft personnel had dramatically risen in popularity. At this juncture, as far as I know, only one of the safety consultant advocates of the BBS process have pushed for a Zero Injury mind set. Instead with most consultants, BBS pushes for a Zero At-Risk Behavior concept. This is a "leading indicator" approach and obviously an improved means of measuring safety in a workplace over a lagging indicator such as worker injury frequency.

There are various methods of incorporating BBS into a work group but basically it begins with the identification of a list of "at risk" behaviors that, if used, will likely result in injury. Job site audits are used to gage the percentage of "at risk" behaviors versus "safe" behavior. The object, of course, is to continually increase the percentage of safe behaviors over at risk behaviors.

With BBS, when you begin to involve the workers, you are not just trying to lower injury rates. You are trying to do something specific that prevents injury; that is "upstream," if you will, of the occurrence of an injury.

The application of these processes are effective and have proven to be a valid methodology in altering the workers' willingness to use "at-risk" behavior in executing their work. Some of these BBS processes utilize the workers themselves in measuring their own "at-risk" behavior. Others use the foremen to do the observations. If you retain one of these consultants, they train you and your employees to measure a project customized list of "safe" and "at-risk" behaviors.

Then, by spreading the BBS process to greater numbers of employees and thus observations, one can, in time, reduce dramatically the number of instances where employees are observed using "at-risk" behavior in accomplishing their work assignments. These measured results are posted where the employees can actually see the progress they are making. Typical reporting would show a chart of "Percent Safe Work." Percentages of "safe work" ranging up to and above 95 percentile are desired. Some achieve percentages "safe work" exceeding 99%.

BBS is gaining in popularity. There are videos, training materials, and software available from several of these proponents to assist you in applying this technology to your workplace. In a recent Internet search for BBS I found over 200 Internet Web sites that used the words in the material found by the search engine. So, from this little piece of exploration, one can see where the current attention is being focused.

The BBS approach is just what it advertises to be; that is a worker involvement tool. It is viable, good and powerful if used with the proper amount of training and utilization of the application processes and if BBS is completely supported by management. The key words in the preceding sentence are "completely supported."

For behavior based safety support to be institutionalized, the managers and supervisors will need training as well. While BBS techniques are viable, as with any other technique, they must be properly structured and applied for successful long term injury reduction to be the result. I like the BBS products and think the application to be a powerful worker involvement process.

Remember, worker focused Behavior Based Safety can be rendered invalid if management does not have its own safety thinking structured and its safety "commitment" well defined.

The 2002 Findings

The CII "Making Zero Accidents Happen" Taskforce also performed research in the process industries where the operating units are subjected to periodic maintenance. These short duration maintenance efforts (frequently including capital additions and expansions) are called "Unit Shutdowns," "Unit Turnarounds" or "Unit Outages." I will use the term "Shutdown" to discuss the research results.

The unique and challenging feature of a Shutdown is that it has extremely rapid build up of activities and thus employees. As opposed to a much slower build up in the average construction project, a Shutdown presents a host of challenges not found in the average longer-term construction project. Seven-day workweeks, with 10 to 12 hour shifts are common. Detailed pre-planning of all phases of the work, including the pre-shutdown planning of the safety aspects of the work and the work processes is of vital importance.

The Taskforce did the research on 44 Process industry Shutdowns in Petro-Chemical, Paper, Power and other Industrial facilities. Amazingly, 22 of these Shutdowns, were executed with Zero OSHA Recordable injuries. Also, of the 44, 38 were completed with Zero Lost Time injuries.

It goes without saying, that these contractors are the best of the best with the Recordable Incident Rate averaging 0.70 for all 44 Shutdowns.

The Taskforce wanted to determine what, if any, specific worker management techniques were used by those contractors that achieved Zero Recordable injuries in executing these Shutdowns.

   The key research areas were:
   1. People resources
   2. Planning

The Zero Injury Guide Book

3. Scheduling
4. Contract formation strategy covers safety
5. Degree of support of CII's Zero Accidents research

People –
- Bringing workers in 2 weeks before or sooner
  - Those who did RIR = 0.22
  - Those who did not RIR = 0.58

- Workers brought in that were familiar with the work
  - Those who did RIR = 0.47
  - Those who did not RIR = 2.28

Planning –
- Software used to schedule work
  - Those who did RIR = 0.72
  - Those who did not RIR = 2.92

- Schedule unit used to plan work
  - Days RIR = 1.51
  - Shifts RIR = 0.68
  - Hours RIR = 0.45

- Days worked per week
  - Seven RIR = 0.96
  - Six RIR = 0.38

- Shutdown duration
  - Two to eight weeks RIR = 1.20
  - Less than two weeks RIR = 0.62

- Crew size
  - Over 12 workers RIR = 1.62
  - Seven or less RIR = 0.55

Combination of People and Planning approach
- Worker familiar and scheduled by hour
  - Not familiar/hours not used RIR = 1.75
  - Familiar or Hours RIR = 1.08
  - Familiar AND Hours RIR = 0.28

Combination Planning and Scheduling
- Duration and Days worked
  - Four weeks at 7 days RIR = 1.36
  - Less than two weeks and six days RIR = 0.38

The Zero Injury Guide Book

Contract Strategy
- Contract Incentivized for Zero Injury
  - No incentive RIR = 1.73
  - Yes to incentive RIR = 0.71
  - Craft get Incentives RIR = even better than 0.71
  - All get incentive if RIR = 0.00
  - No one gets incentive if there is a recordable
  - Incentives awarded on weekly performance

An interesting and powerful safety motto for all on the shutdown was given by a Taskforce member was as follows:

"If it is not safe I will not do it and will not let others do it."

Such a motto really speaks to the heart of a Zero Injury culture where "every man is a safetyman." All have a fearless devotion to seeing the work completed without an injury to anyone.

The Taskforce further stated that the shutdowns that performed at the Zero Recordable Rate were only those that used the above approach to managing the work along with the use of all nine of the Zero Accident techniques given on page 71.

Chapter 11 – Author's Recommendations

Critical Implementation Priorities

From my observations of successes and failures over 12 years of consulting I offer the following critical recommendations to those seeking Zero Injury as a working cultural norm in their companies.

1. Nothing is more important than an intense "passion" for "zero injury" at the very top – CEO/COO-management level in the company! Talk the safety talk. And "WALK" the safety talk! Being committed, as CEO, to zero injury means that little sleep comes on nights following an injury to one of your employees. When that sleepless night happens, then you know you are committed. It is then you begin to realize that injury to one of your employees has become "unacceptable."

Think of this definition of "commitment" on the part of top leaders.

> "If your rest pattern is not disturbed by the fact that an injury occurred to one of your employees then you may need to work on your definition of your commitment to the safety of your employees."

2. Remember your people will take chances out of a sense of loyalty if you do not spell out your zeal for "zero accidents." The top leaders must make it clear to all that "risk taking" in the interest of production, schedule, or cost is not acceptable.

3. Set the expectation of Zero Injuries in your company. Management will need to meet with the employees and explain why. Enlist your employee's participation. Use employee involvement processes.

4. Insure foremen and other line management are totally responsible for safety performance. Safety professionals are advisors only and are extremely important. Have them

working on safety compliance, safety training and conducting safety inspections and audits. The successful companies are holding line management accountable for safety performance.

5. Every meeting of the senior management and lower management groups, always begin with emphasis on the safety performance of the company.

6. Routine and frequent reports of the safety performance status are given the CEO. When the CEO is asked how long it has been since the last injury you always get a definitive answer! When speaking to groups of employees he never forgets to speak on safety as his opening subject.

7. Insure that all people, at all levels, understand that safety is of paramount importance; that it is a value, thus not subject to prioritization and certainly never should be merely co-equal with production. Many of those who embrace the Zero Injury concept say that the Zero Injury Initiative actually improves production. And all those who reach zero recordable injury say that those are the projects that are the most profitable as well.

8. Expect that accident and injury reporting be done by management and be immediate and have the highest profile. For instance, the CEO gets an immediate personal call from a selected management level when a lost workday injury occurs.

9. Set up a job site visit by senior level executives of both contractor and owner, occurring no later than the day following a lost workday case, to review what occurred and plan management steps to prevent further deterioration of safety performance.

10. Have an innovative safety program in place that is in a continuous state of improvement at all times. Continuous

improvement keeps the program before the employees and keeps their attention.

11. Consider the use of recognition rewards for safe behavior performance. Insure that it is group performance focused. Recognition for "zero" injury achievement must be given attention by the highest level of management. Routine means of recognition must be developed. Monthly recognition when zero injury is occurring is a good idea with intermediate milestone and annual awards for achievement also routine. The Owner or CEO passes out the annual awards!! This can take the form of a celebration dinner with spouses invited. Now you are walking the safety talk!

Far too often I see employers achieve zero injury and fail to recognize, some times, at all and sometimes too long after the event took place.

Track your performance carefully and recognize the achievement of zero injury and make it timely!

12. Develop means to insure the costs of safety non-performance (injuries) are charged to each project or department before the profit or loss is calculated. These charges may have to be estimates early on. Include any corporate level indirect costs. Such a system clearly tells the manager who is ultimately responsible for injury and that managers will carry their own injury burdens.

13. Insure that line management down through the foreman to the worker level, is at least annually evaluated on safety performance along with the other critical evaluation factors.

14. If subcontractors are involved, screen your bid list and require well run safety programs and a commitment to zero injury from them as well. Sub-contractors always show up with the appropriate personal protective equipment.

The Zero Injury Guide Book

15. Utilize first day, in depth, safety and job orientation of all new hires on construction jobs. This is a good time for new hires to meet the project management personnel who can use this time to impart to the new employees a sense of urgency in maintaining a "zero" injury performance level. Insisting that Managers participate in the new employee orientation is how you communicate the zero expectation to the worker.

16. Train employees in safe work habits. Formally.

17. Train foremen and superintendents in supervisory skills and safety. Insure they buy in to the zero injury expectation. Also hold these line managers of safe production accountable for any injury that occurs. They must report up the line, even if the information has preceded their call via the safety representative reporting chain.

18. Refer to the Construction Industry Institute Zero Accident Research products. The results of the 1993 and 2001 and 2002 research are available.

19. It is very important to insure that Line Management take on the responsibility and accountability for a safe workplace and a safe work process. In fact, the leader of a safety function in a company should be named the Safety Director rather than Safety Manager, to prevent the idea that somehow the Safety function "manages" safety. Insure that "safety management" is first and always a line management function.

Caution urged for Monetary Safety Incentives

Monetary incentives seem to have an attraction that is deceptive. Some want to use incentives first, hoping that this money will somehow persuade employees to work injury free. This is but one of the problems opponents see in the use of this technique. If you do decide to use incentives, do so only after you have successfully incorporated all the other Zero Injury techniques into your safety management process. In my experience it is a proven fact that safety incentives in absence of any proactive use of the proven zero injury techniques will cause employees to under-report injuries.

This is the reason also that the use of safety incentives in cash form has found disfavor in many quarters. The argument is that such incentives will, even if inadvertently on the part of the employer, lead employees to hide injury. As a result OSHA has launched an inquiry into the "hiding injury" claim.
However, many contractors remain faithful users of the monetary safety incentive technique. All that do, use incentives very selectively on projects with start and end dates. I currently know of no companies that attempt to use monetary incentives on the lagging indicator of injury frequency on a company wide basis.

If used, incentives should always be used on an interdependent, employee to employee format where all work to win the award or no one wins it. The object, of course, is to get all employees enlisted in the effort to cause interemployee communications about working safely to reach a very high level.

There are contractors who simply will not use cash incentives because they are firmly against them in principal. Many that oppose monetary incentives are also found achieving remarkable safety records. There is, of course the opposing argument that properly managed monetary incentives do a very effective job is helping employees keep their mind on safety.

For an in-depth look at the pro and con of incentives see the Appendix, Item 2 – page 166.

PART 2

THE DETAILS OF A CONTINUOUS IMPROVEMENT PROCESS

Chapter 12 - Taking Management Action

First Things First – A Detailed Approach

Delegating the management of safety does not mean relegating leadership to lower levels of management. Safety leadership must be held and directed from the top levels of management.

One of the challenges facing Top Management, however, is that of alignment on the commitment and action required to achieve a Zero Injury working culture. Such alignment can be achieved through a facilitated workshop where the Top Management group is guided through a process that allows alignment to occur. It would be beneficial if this workshop were preceded by an in-depth explanation of the Zero Injury concept, its origins and the logic supporting the Concept along with examples of those who are successful.

Properly managed safety, as I have pointed out, does not lower productivity; rather using the CII Research results in managing safety can improve productivity. However it is often found that lower level managers typically do not readily accept this improved productivity concept. The reason is that it is strange to the currently in-place common culture of "pushing production" that has ruled the workplace in America for the past 100 plus years.

Thus, it is incumbent on company upper management to lead the Zero Injury culture revolution to insure change does, in fact, take place.

Once the safety commitment has been examined in-depth and redefined, the next step is to flesh out the safety program incorporating the CII Best Practices. The following is a list of important leadership initiatives.

They are –
1. **Establish a Corporate Safety Committee** CSC
    a. Led by the CEO.
        The agenda is changing the safety culture.
    b. Conduct a culture change workshop to develop a prioritized agenda.
    c. Conduct regular and frequent meetings on how the prioritized agenda is to be implemented.

2. **Embrace Behavior Based Safety for the Manager cadre**.
    a. Design a corporate accountability model.
        i. Who reports to whom when an injury occurs?
        ii. Who investigates injuries?
        iii. Who is responsible for corrective action?
        iv. How soon and when are investigations conducted?
        v. Who reviews the investigation reports?
        vi. Share the investigation results!

3. **Install an injury management program**.
    a. Develop a Physician liaison process.
        i. Create a Physician and medical service network.
    b. Develop return to work policy.
        i. Include a "Restricted Duty" capability.
    c. Assign responsibility for maintaining injured worker contacts.
    d. Assign responsibility for insurance carrier interface.
        i. Audit injury reserves.
        ii. Close cases as quickly as possible, insuring the injured has recovered.

4. **Develop safety teams at lower management levels as the organizational structure indicates**. Insure that these safety teams are linked. The leader of the teams just below the Corporate Safety Committee is a member of the CSC. Link lower level teams to the one above in like manner.
    a. The agenda for these safety teams is the

management of safety, setting safety action goals and guiding the culture change process.
   b. Conducting zero injury workshops to create the prioritized agenda for each team is important.
5. Institute a "Top down guideline, "bottom up" goal setting process." (This process is discussed in detail in the pages following.)

Defining Safety Goals

These goals set by each safety team (see Chapter 16, 17 and the appendix for more on Safety Teams) are not just classical goals for some number of injuries as tradition would have it. Rather they are the goals for CII Zero Injury safety technique implementation. The safety techniques found most powerful in the CII research were (See Chapter 9 and 10 for details):

- Demonstrated management commitment
- Staffing for safety
- Safety planning
    o Pre-Project planning
    o Pre-Task planning
- Safety training and education
    o Safety Orientation
    o Formal Safety training
- Worker participation and involvement
    o Safety teams
    o Behavior Based Safety training
- Recognition and rewards
    o Monthly
- Subcontractor management
    o Screen
- Accident/incident reporting and investigations
    o Emphasize near miss/hit tracking
    o Communicate results of investigations
- Drug and alcohol testing

Chapter 13 - The Process That Yields Evergreen Safety Progress

Creating an Integrated Safety Management System
Now that you have the background information and safety techniques and the detailed approach to be used to achieve success, let's review an employee-involvement Safety Team process.

As stated earlier, all the work in the world will not yield the result of Zero Injury unless you have a process that involves the employees.

Not involving the employees is the traditional approach to safety management. Those achieving success today in eliminating injury are using employee involvement processes. I have discussed Behavior Based Safety above. Now I will cover in more detail "safety teams," for that is where my experience has been.

The Safety Team is a process that, if followed, will lead you and your organization to that coveted goal of "Zero Injury." It is a pathway that has been blazed by others. The landmarks are clear. Such a path is revealed in the following pages.

While one will find a few references to specific works by others, the information for this book, in addition to the author's personal experience, has been countless sources on the subject of managing safety. These data sources have been integrated throughout four decades of practical application, and in the last few years, took on the present form of what is termed in the book as an "integrated safety management system".

Few companies bother to use an "integrated system" approach to safety management. Most seem to use a series of tools, or sub-systems, that manage safety plans, techniques, costs, production, and completion schedules. All these are needed, but there is a failure to integrate the skills of the workforce, in an optimum systematic fashion, to ensure a mode of "automatic safety progress" that is pervasive and ongoing.

Automatic Safety Progress

Those that install the system explained herein can acquire that illusive competitive edge of "excellence" that typifies those that are the best in their business: those whose employees are rarely injured.

The "safety management system" presented to you in the following pages is not a theory on how to manage safety. Rather it is a proven system, tried and tested prior to being recorded here. It is not a quick fix; rather, it is a permanent fix.

The system installation process takes time and hard work. However, once you have the system in place, your "safety management search" will be over. You will be well down the path of acquiring the feeling of achievement that goes with a Zero Injury working culture.

This safety management process does incorporate many of the management techniques and tools espoused by various safety management authors during the last twenty years. Those included are techniques and tools that work, not only in principle, but in fact.

The approach used in this book recognizes that most skilled managers do not have time to read a mountain of information to get the essence of a subject, nor do they want an excess of help. They are anxious to use their own talents and innovation in filling in the fine details of how to design and implement a system.

Thus, the object of this book is to describe the broad basics of this proven safety management process in almost an outline form. You will find the system elements described in brief fashion with the attendant sacrifice of a lot of fine detail.

I do not try to overwhelm you with persuasive arguments. A little logic is presented and then the system element. Herein are the bare elements of a proven effective safety management process that produces the elimination of injury "automatically."

"Automatic" does not mean that no effort or energy is required. To the contrary, a lot of energy will be required to install and implement the system. The important thing about this energy, however, is that it brings about progress. And in today's competitive business world, one must make significant progress on a continual basis in order to remain in a competitive position in the market place.

People Involvement
Involving your people in the creative safety management process is where "the system" derives its strength. Safety Teams are formed to address safety issues and solving the question "How do we become a Zero Injury culture." These teams involve more than just your managerial and supervisory cadre; they also involve all your people, including any on an hourly payroll.

Embarking on a "safety team people involvement" process is best if done as a part of a long-term commitment. Long term is because, once experienced by your people, the mass of them will become so devoted to the process that leaders can demoralize their organization if they to revert to a totally authoritarian style.

The fact is, you will not want to revert for you will see the power and the resulting world-class safety performance. If you take the commitment to utilize safety teams, do so with the knowledge that, in many respects, it is a "one-way path." It is, however, a "one way path" to Zero Injury. A worthy end!

Having experienced the feeling of achievement that results from being a part of the installation of an "integrated safety management process," and having shared the resulting rewards, it seems mandatory to the author that the system be recorded for others to use.

Good luck! It is hard work, but the results will be worth it.

Choosing A Name for the Organization (for this book)
Enterprises that can benefit from the installation of a safety management process come in many shapes and sizes. In general, the "names" of these "work places" or "work efforts" come in an equal number of choices.

For instance, the following are a few of the names that apply to these places or enterprises: shop, mill, company, office, firm, corporation, department, division, region, project, staff, mine, facility, factory, store, refinery, bureau and plant. "Facility" was chosen to identify the "work place" referenced in this book because it was in a manufacturing facility that the system was proven. The point in selecting a name is unimportant other than to point out that where people gather in an organized fashion to pursue a common objective in our "working" world varies and does not matter in the final analysis.

The presentation of the conceptual elements of the "integrated safety management system" is done in Chapter 16 using just ten steps and is free of extensive, in-depth explanations. This does not mean that the various distinct aspects of the safety management process presented fail to embody a degree of complexity.

During the author's experience in installing the system, a multitude of questions were generated by those involved that required answers. As these questions surfaced, they were typically answered via articles written for wide in-facility distribution. Rather than include all that detail in the body of the book, those articles have been appended. Each deals with a variety of questions that go beyond the content implied by the title.

Chapter 14 - Safety Management System Evolution

The Beginning
Since the beginning of the Industrial Revolution, managers have been learning how to manage safety. One observation seems to reflect the nature of the evolution of safety management expertise.

> "That which worked yesterday somehow is not quite adequate for today."

Safety management professionals have continually worked on the latest applications of the most advanced theories. Volumes, and more volumes, keep pouring out of printing presses. Recently, the subject has been Behavior Based Safety. Most all is extremely good material, along with concepts with which to work, but none give the answer sought on how to achieve "evergreen" progress.

There also seems to be a recent correlation that reflects that the more brief, succinctly ("One Minute" & "Idiot's Guide") written materials win large enthusiastic management followings. I have not seen a publication named "The Dummies Guide to Safety Management." But wait awhile, it seems there is one for any conceivable challenge. In time, someone will publish something on safety with such a title.

What seems to be lacking in publications available today on safety management is a process that integrates all the material available. Lacking is an overall plan that assembles this mass of method into a "system" one can use to make progress. An "integrated process for safety management" is needed that allows the broader spectrum of the management challenge to be effectively addressed.

In dealing with the challenges we managers frequently face, we run to our safety management toolbox and find that we really do not need a specific tool, but a way to simultaneously use many tools.

Therefore, it seems to me we are in need of "a safety management process"; a safety management process that, once present in the organization, will yield progress in reducing "at-risk" behavior on a continuous (automatic and ever-green) basis.

It is not merely the same progress that we now strive for in an authoritative fashion. It is an even higher level of progress that a well-integrated safety management system, using people involvement, will automatically give you.

In fact, this "progress" to which I refer can become so automatic that, once you have the system working, you will sometimes find yourself watching in amazement.

Chapter 15 - Safety Management Choices

Zero Injury Team Choices

In the technological and industrial world we live in, many options exist on how to manage safety in an enterprise. To achieve a Zero Injury working culture, the really important team choices are made early.

The team decisions you will need to make are influenced by two basic situations.

One, you have a short-term management challenge, such as a project where you need to involve people at all levels in creating the Zero Injury safety culture.

Two, you have a more long-term situation where there will be low employee turnover. In this later case there are again two sets of circumstances.

One, this is a new facility; these are new people and the opportunities on how to structure the "people" part of managing safety are almost endless.

Two, this is an existing facility; these are in-place people and the opportunities are, at best, limited on how to devise a safety management system with which to work.

If your situation is the first, you can enlarge your staff by hiring a safety professional or, if you choose the more temporary route, you can retain a safety consultant and carefully design your beginnings in safety management with teams. You are indeed blessed. If you heed sound advice, your success with safety team management can almost be assured.

This implementation section has much information for you within its pages, and you can use it while you do the basics

The Zero Injury Guide Book

on how you want to involve your employees in achieving the Zero Injury culture you desire. A few choices are Teams, Quality Circles, and Self-directed work groups. What will it be? You'll still need a sound safety management process, but you can do the structural basics simultaneously.

If your situation is the second described above, "this is an existing facility, these are in-place people and my structural opportunities are limited---" this book also has much for you.

Looking at this second type of work place, on the surface, your people seem to do the tasks they are assigned fairly safely. These tasks have become "their" jobs. You sense they do their jobs well and they want to be left alone. But you find injuries occurring. You wonder why?

As boss you agree. "Let me leave them alone," you say as you think this through. "They will be happier, they will get the job done and I'll be happy," but if only we can achieve a shift to the better in safety performance.

Lets' say you do wait, thinking it through, looking for options. In fact, you do it well. But after a while you notice your people simply aren't making progress in safety; at least, not enough to meet the competition in the market place, and satisfy your own high standards to be the best.

At this point you may be tempted to intervene. "I'll ask for more safety focus," you think. But deep inside you know there isn't much more focus to be given. You fear if you push much more for more, you'll get less: because, due to the pressure from you, your people may start to do unwise things that will result in increased injury; not less. You want them to think of safety as part of production. You want them to realize that improved safety will not sacrifice production, but will actually improve production to be safe production!

The Zero Injury Guide Book

It is likely that if you told them this last fact, they would not believe you. Somehow, you want to create a process that will, in it-self, prove your position without their being told. A way needed to improve safety so, when it is over, they will realize that productivity, was not sacrificed but rather was improved.

Faced with this challenge and your experience, you have been to the safety toolbox many times in the past, and tried many programs. It seemed that some helped, but soon the place was back to needing another safety technique; another shot in the arm.

How then can one make this progress toward Zero Injury, in a situation like this?

The answer is simple: Get help.

You ask, "Get Help? I thought we were leaving the tradition behind," you answer. Help from whom?"

You have asked the key question: from whom?

If I told you to ask for help from all those from whom you are reluctant to ask for more; those that are doing their job and doing it well, but leaving safety behind too many times; what would you say? - or ask?

Perhaps your question is "How can I do this?" If you sincerely have this question in your mind, then, you are ready to start down the path to safety progress to an even higher safety performance level termed "automatic safety progress" that will guarantee your future as a Zero Injury culture.

Chapter 16 – The Safety Management System

There Are Ten Steps
The Safety Management System consists of ten steps that if followed faithfully will accelerate your chances for rapid progress toward the establishment of a Zero Injury culture where worker injury is a rare event.

These ten steps are:
1. Setting the Safety Foundation
2. Getting Help for your Safety Culture Change
3. Using the Safety Team Help Process
4. Creating Safety Action Goals
5. Using System Operational Guidelines
6. Using the Safety Goals Review Process
7. Capturing the Progress as Evergreen
8. Working Out Relationships
9. Making Quality Part of the Process
10. Invoking Progress Now!

STEP ONE –

SETTING THE SAFETY FOUNDATION

The Most Important Ingredient

Most managers today agree that the most important ingredient of an enterprise is not the hardware, nor the money but the people. One could call the facilities and equipment the foundation.

This simply recognizes that the very latest in facility equipment with plenty of money will not automatically yield safety success. These are essential but the paramount "key" to the success of your enterprise in safety, to reaching the coveted Zero Injury performance and yielding automatic progress is in how well your people function in recognizing and avoiding "at-risk" behavior.

This being the case, then you will need to spend significant time examining and rethinking how your employees are treated as a part of a revised Zero Injury safety management effort.

Start With The Basics

We'll start with the basics, the safety management foundation, if you will. One cannot build a lasting structure upon an ill designed or inadequate foundation. Where or how then can we find the material for this foundation? Since we are going to consider basics in creating this safety management system we will need to consider the fundamental purpose of the facility we have.

Let's call this "fundamental purpose", the facility mission. What is the mission; what commodity, service, product or products is this facility supposed to produce; and with what broad perspectives in mind? In addition, consideration is required to how you wish your people to function including their individual health and welfare.

It is recognized that, in some cases, the "mission" definition has been written by some other higher authority. Your job as leader of a sub-group is to guide your people in adopting the higher mission statement and operating within its boundaries. The following information is for those who are in a "mission creation mode."

Have you made it very clear in any mission statement you have in place that employee safety is of paramount importance. Is it clear to the employees that you are not the least interested in making a profit at the expense of their well being? Is it clearly stated in your mission statement that an injury to any employee is simply not an acceptable event in the course of performing their work?

"Oh, that's obvious," you say, "everyone knows that." Well, if everyone knows, why then can we not continue to make the safety progress that we need to remain competitive? Why do employees insist on taking shortcuts and utilizing "at-risk" behavior in order to accomplish their tasks? Might these "at risk" behaviors have management's tacit approval?

So bear with me. Think a restated mission that includes employee safety as a major aspect of a successful corporate cultural change effort. Think of it in terms that use 100 words or less. Think of it in broad terms, not in great detail. We'll get to the detail later.

Mission Statement Includes Safety

Create the Mission statement draft and include appropriate references to safety so that the value tenets covered become the underpinning of your organization. You might even want to, indeed you should, involve your immediate management group to help you create this statement. Use the group that reports directly to you. After all, they need to experience this thought process also. Together you address the question "What is our corporate commitment to safety? Are we only "really committed?" Or are we going to be committed to the point that "it is not acceptable for an injury to occur."

Remember that this Mission statement you are about to create is the foundation on which you are going to build this safety management system. It must be a statement that you believe and support and are willing to publish for all to have. And just as importantly, you are prepared to "live by the mission words." What belongs in The Mission Statement? Use simple statements. Include the basics.

For instance:

> "The XYZ Company's purpose is to produce the best 'Zaphs' on the market. Zaphs manufactured here will appeal to our customers and fulfill their expectations.
>
> In order to accomplish this we wish to create a working culture where it is clear that our employees are our most valuable asset, and our customers our most important concern. Thus it will be important in our mission to protect this employee asset against injury or abuse. Since employee injury is not an acceptable event in XYZ Company we desire and will strive to create a working culture where there are zero injuries to our employees. In so doing we feel we can more properly serve our customers.
>
> We also wish to conserve our facility asset. All should recognize that in order to secure our stockholder's investment in the facilities, and our employees continued employment that a profit is the anticipated result of our efforts."

Be honest. In a free enterprise system, motives are known

anyway. Spell out the important relationships that need to exist. It is the information contained in the Mission statement that will become the common safety objective that will bind you and your people together as you travel this newfound pathway to an injury free culture.

Set Your Working Climate

A safe working climate (safe working environment) is of paramount importance. When your people know what their collective "mission" is, they also need to know something of your broad expectations regarding the "safe working environment." Most leaders, by not sharing with the employees their visions regarding safety leave this important "workplace condition" to chance.

The benefit of thinking through the elements of a "safe working environment" tends to solidify how one acts around the workplace. Developing a "Safe Working Environment" as a part of the overall Mission document commits the leaders to certain safe behavioral and management norms that they individually and as a group must consciously support.

Some have called this an "organizational climate for safety." This desired safe working environment, or climate, needs to be defined and written also, again for all to see. This should be no more than a one-page document that describes the "people considerations" that you as the leader would like to see as work place norms.

For instance:
- Employees will have opportunity to gain personal safety information to help them in avoiding "at-risk" behavior.
- Employees will reflect a friendly and cooperative attitude toward their peers as they work on a safe workplace together.
- Safety information needed to perform the tasks to be done will be available when required.

- An attitude of "pride in safety" will be prevalent in the facility.

Most of the lists I have seen contain 12 to 15 statements of similar nature.

You can look at the Safe Working Climate document as a loose framework of safety norms that you would like to see in your company or operational segment. If at all possible it is important to allow your employees to be a part of the creation of such a list. If they are involved in the creation process, the safety norms will be largely in place when the document is finished. Otherwise, it will take time for the work force to adopt those safety norms created by others as their own.

The Zero Injury Guide Book

STEP TWO –

GETTING HELP FOR YOUR SAFETY CULTURE CHANGE

Making Progress
Progress never comes without change. You can print it, frame it and hang it on the wall. It's true, has always been true and always will be true. Accept the fact.

Progress never comes without effort. You can work doubly hard and drag more "effort" out of everyone or, better still, you can get this extra effort to voluntarily flow.

Progress never comes without involvement. If you mandate progress, the people affected are involved. If you catalyze voluntary effort, you also get voluntary involvement. And I ask you this, "Which is more powerful; mandated involvement of voluntary involvement?"

Think "change, effort and involvement."

Then think of "how." How do I instill in the people on whom I now depend an "attitude" that will yield automatic safety progress?

You do not do it by telling them that they need a new safety attitude. It is not a "telling" they need.

You start by "asking". But, it is very, very important that you ask in the right way and that your reasons for asking have a sound logical base.

The Nature of People
In order to develop this sound logical base, let's deal with the nature of people. Research has shown that it is the nature of people to want to be involved to some degree in the decisions

that are made that affect their work, work place safety, and the work product.

To begin with then, we must realize that to "ask" is to "involve." When people become involved they expect some degree of response to their answers to the asking.

So you must use a process to involve people that "asks" them in the right way and that will deal with the responses they give in a responsible manner that gives them feedback.

What kind of process? What are my options, you ask?

The Zero Injury Guide Book

STEP THREE –

USING THE "SAFETY TEAM" HELP PROCESS

Automatic Evergreen Progress

Remember, you are working toward a safety management process that yields "automatic evergreen progress." So when you take a step toward installing a part of this safety management system, remember that it is not a "one-shot" effort. What you do is not only for now but for the future as well.

You are going to develop a system that is integrated, in place and yielding progress. You also want progress despite the periodic perturbations that face the organization, a new government safety regulation to meet, a new product or product safety specification to meet, or a change in safety staff from time to time.

So the Help Process that you create should be one that continues, evergreen in nature, and which is flexible enough to manage necessary change. The current safety management toolbox contains a number of "involvement" options; Quality Circles, Task Teams, Safety Teams, and Behavior Based Safety, to name four.

Quality Circles have been used to involve employees in a quality of product sense, in a quality of work life sense and a safety sense.

Task Teams usually have a finite life and address a specific "short term" issue.

Safety Teams

Safety Teams are an employee involvement process that shows strong promise for the long term. "Teaming" safety is a employee empowering process that allows employees to set their own safety goals, from the bottom (crafts/workers) up. (Not injury goals, but goals in how to work with less "at-risk" behavior.)

When one considers teams please realize teams can have considerable variation in sophistication.

In safety, one can begin with a very elementary team. Elementary safety teams are recommended for a short term workforce or one with high turnover rates. Sophisticated safety teams require more meeting time and investment of team training thus are recommended for a more permanent workforce.

STEP FOUR –

CREATING SAFETY ACTION GOALS

How To Create Goals

Knowing "how to use" a Safety Goals Program is just as important as creating the program. A Safety Goals Program will often yield little, if any, progress if the program isn't used in the right way.

It is productive to set up an understanding on the meaning of and use of the words "Mission", "Objective" and "Goal." My suggestion is that "Mission" be the overriding and guiding document that allows "Objectives" to be set that are aimed at achieving the mission. Specific "Goals" are then set to accomplish an "Objective." Each "Goal" will have specific "action steps" that give assignment of responsibility for an action or actions. Action steps are given completion dates designed to accomplish the goals in a timely manner.

Let's talk about the "nature of people" again. When it comes to people and goals there are two kinds of situations.

In the first situation, the leaders develop goals and pass them down to the employees. These are top-down goals while usually accepted as "how 'they' do it around here," such goals very frequently have only half-hearted support from those effected and the level of commitment, which might seem satisfactory from afar, when viewed up close is found to be vague and uncertain. Questions from the employees sound like "How could they arrive at such a goal; don't they know what's going on down here?"

The above underlined words are the key explanations of the problem. They, they, and down. Passed "down" from "up there."

In the second situation we find "the way" to implement a safety goals program. This "bottom-up" method will often yield more stringent employee safety goals with attendant higher performance results than could be exacted with a "tops down" approach.

Management Gives Safety Goal Guidelines Only!

Start by thinking "Tops Down Safety Guidelines" - not goals: only guidelines. These guidelines will be the "direction setters" for your progress. They need not be, but can be "Objectives;" such as "It is Management's desire that we create a Zero Injury Culture in our facility." In each area that you desire progress, include in the Safety Goal Guidelines statements to that effect, i.e. Guideline:

1. Each safety team is to develop its own safety mission statement toward the achievement of a Zero Injury work team.

2. Each safety team will set stretch safety goals that call for implementation and adherence to safe work techniques.

3. Each safety team will set stretch safety goals that will reduce the amount of "at-risk" behavior found in the execution of work procedures and processes.

4. Each safety team will develop goals that will result in improved knowledge in safe working skills and team skills.

5. Each safety team will forecast, for budgeting purposes, the expected training required to accomplish its' safety goals, including any capital expense.

You might ask, "But what about costs? Won't they skyrocket? How can I, as leader, on the one hand give people the responsibility to set safety goals, some of which obviously cost money and at the same time contain the potential cost explosion?"

Do this too with guidelines. Note in your cover letter what the business climate is, how profits have looked and ask for help.

There are many ways to increase profits while not sacrificing safety. Often your people may spend more in one area and reduce costs even more in another area. For instance, it is known that serious injuries cost the employee and the employer a lot money. Thus, if by safety training, injury to employees is reduced then the training expenditure will be more than recovered by reduced employee suffering and medical expense.

Finally, in your guidelines letter inform those who are setting goals, that management at a level higher than the team leader will <u>review</u> the team goals at the outset of the new fiscal year and then quarterly thereafter.

It is also a good idea to set these dates for the quarterly reviews in advance so your people can arrange their calendars to be available on those dates. To not set the dates risks an ineffective review process due to absences of key personnel..

STEP FIVE –

USING THE SYSTEM OPERATIONAL GUIDELINES

The Key to Automatic Progress
The key to putting your "automatic progress" system on automatic is in the holding of "Safety Goals Reviews." Reviews give you the opportunity to influence safety goals in their early state: to keep up on safety technique implementation progress, new developments and new safety issues. Reviews put you in close contact with the safety action on a regular basis and through careful questioning that you can gently guide.

Developing Guidelines
Allow me to structure the Guidelines, Goals, and Review process in a chronological manner. Do not be deceived. The entire Guidelines, Goals, and Review processes require a lot of time and energy. But it is time and energy that is specifically dealing with that which you desire most: a Zero Injury Company, and such a company is tantamount to "safety excellence."

Spending time on safety goals is time well spent. To not spend this time, means you are choosing to remain in a stifled, no-progress, mode dealing with the problems of today in a reactionary manner as you have in the past.

What you must do to convert from "reactionary" safety management to "pro-active" safety management is to adopt a safety management system embodying a goals and review process.

When the people in your organization set their goals, they will necessarily address dealing with all the problems they face everyday. As these problems are dealt with, solutions are found and problems that have been historic go away. The time thus available can then be spent on preventing or setting up a structure to deal with the problems of tomorrow. You are, at this point, moving from a "reactive" to a "pro-active" safety management mode.

The chronology of your approach is very important. Start by issuing "top down guidelines." Select the time of year you wish all goals to be created, re-examined, updated, dropped or added. A few months prior to this, publish your guidelines. Include in your annual guidelines cover letter any philosophies or developments in the business that you wish to pass along to your safety goal developers.

When operating in a Safety Team mode your sub-leaders develop their departmental or functional goals in concert with their involved people. This process is begun by everyone developing ideas for their own individual work-related team safety goals, then bringing them to the larger work group "safety goal setting" meeting. At this sub-leader meeting resolution is reached on the group goals.

The sub-leader safety goals become the material from which the next level up, team's safety goals are formulated. It will sometimes be necessary to add the broader group multi-effort goals to the list. For instance foremen will bring their crew team goals to the meeting and those goals may include suggestions for a multi-foreman effort on safety in some critical arena. This then is addressed at the next organizational level.

Guideline Content
Your annual guidelines should include all the broad areas out of the Mission Statement for which you wish Objectives and Goals to be established. A suggested breakdown might include some of the following:
- Safety Objective
- New Safety Goals

- Ongoing Safety Goals
- Safety Planning
- Safety Training
- Safety Compliance issues
- Safety Team Effectiveness

Further breakdown with specific guideline statements can be in order under each of the above topics. For instance, under Safety Goals a guideline statement might be:
 -Each division or department is to conduct a departmental wide safety training seminar each quarter.

Notice that you do not tell them exactly when or what the subject matter need be but you are establishing through the guideline that such a safety seminar is an expected norm. In the goal development process the specific action steps, timing and subject matter for the seminar are determined.

The goal might appear as follows:
Goal:
 Conduct a safety seminar on eye safety with all departmental personnel.

Action:	Timing Mo/Yr	Action by: Indiv.
- Contact "Eye Safety Inc." for program materials	09/01/2003	Joe
- Develop presentation	10/01/2003	Jane
- Arrange for facility	11/01/2003	Jack
- Present seminar	12/01/2003	James

Action steps with timing commitment and responsibilities are extremely important. First, these create logical steps that will yield progress and two, estimates the timing of the progress. To omit action steps and assignments is to slow down progress, perhaps to "no progress."

STEP SIX –

USING THE SAFETY GOALS REVIEW PROCESS

Time Schedule *(April-March Fiscal Year)*
An overall time schedule based on a calendar year might look like this:

Guidelines -	Late November
Goal Setting -	December/March
Reviews:	
Previous year progress -	
Current year goals -	April
First Quarter Review -	July
Second Quarter Review -	
With first six month's results-	October
Develop Guidelines -	November
Guideline letter out -	Late November
Goal Setting -	December/March
Third Quarter Review -	January
Reviews:	
Previous year progress -	
Current year goals -	April

The frequency of the reviews
The quarterly reviews are of paramount importance. If your people, who have set their own goals to your guidelines, are to really believe you are interested in what they are doing, their successes and failures, then "you must review quarterly."

117

To review less often (reflecting lack of interest), you will find less progress. To review more often (too little passage of time), you will find little progress. A so quarterly review works out about right for most situations.

On Automatic

So now you have it on "automatic." All you have to do is insure the Guideline letter is issued and the dates for reviews are established. It is not hard to manage after you get the process going and the momentum is in place.

You and your people will improve with each passing review cycle. The quarterly goal refinements will be added as needed by the teams and "automatic ever-green safety progress" will become second nature.

STEP SEVEN –

CAPTURING THE PROGRESS AS EVERGREEN

Doing it Over and Over
Managers know that the process of managing safety involves doing some things many times over. Safety Procedures to handle many activities, especially those that are complex in nature, need to be developed and systematically documented. These become "Codes of Safe Practice" or "Safety Manuals."

Employee turnover, if nothing else, dictates the productive nature of "documenting the how" of repetitive safety activities. The need to document is especially true where experience has taught that things seem to drop between the chairs and the "I thought you had the action" statements become the response of the day. Most organizations are fairly adept at reducing repetitive items to a procedure. Usually this is done after some recurring difficulty has proved the wisdom of such a step.

From Reactive to Pro-active Management
The pro-active minded organization, that is achieving at the Zero Injury level of performance, will have time to develop a crisis resolution procedure to handle a disruptive event before it occurs. This is especially important in critical safety areas of focus, but is also important in preparing for environmental issues where prevention gets very high priority.

There is a lesson to be learned here that applies throughout an organization. It is productive to develop preventive procedures on many other functional activities. The commonly used procedure of Inventory Control is an illustration of this.

The Zero Injury Guide Book

It is also important to insure that safety procedures, once developed, are given to those who need them, that they are explained (training conducted) and that they are used. Also important is to install a record keeping and filing process that allows safety procedures to be found when they are needed. Such a system should also provide a mechanism for reviewing and updating all safety procedures on a set time interval. Out-of-date safety procedures fall into disuse so it is mandatory to have a review and update process. Sponsors can be assigned each procedure to see that a timely review and re-issue is conducted.

It is also very important that the procedure manuals be assigned specific individuals so when update time arrives a mailing list will get the revised procedure to all those holding copies of the manuals.

STEP EIGHT –

WORKING OUT RELATIONSHIPS

Getting Along Productively

This Step of the management process addresses all relationships and conflicts, not only those that arise out of safety management. Most relationship problems in the work place stem from conflict arising out of "role" understandings or misunderstandings, so these need addressing.

As indicated earlier, it is very, very important to recognize when and where this conflict exists, and to actually put in writing a coordinated role element description for people who must work together to accomplish a common task. The benefits are obvious. Once role elements are reasonably well understood, most work place conflict ceases and that conflict which remains stems from such things as differences in ideology, personality and style.

Human relations research has been done in the field of helping people understand other people. Some theorists feel that the only way to work out understandings between people is through facilitated confrontation. And this is probably true if one considers confrontation as the event where the two (or more) of the people involved get together in order to promote an atmosphere of understanding. Only where rational working relationships are desired, can the people involved create one.

Do Not Try to be a Doctor of Psychology

"Fine tuning" severe relationship problems should not be undertaken by the average "lay" (in the sense of human relation expertise) facilitator. Rather, the troubled parties should seek out specialists with the appropriate training and academic credentials. These "experts" are available in sufficient number and background that one can be located with specific expertise that would fit most any need.

The question should be answered as to whether or not to take this conflict resolution step of "working out relationships." Occasionally, people do learn to work very well together. They see the need to overcome personal differences in style for the good of the enterprise. Developing a conflict solution process, one that fine tunes relationships is a productivity item. If you need to do it, and have not, how can you ask others to become more productive? A good example is the best teacher of all.

STEP NINE –

MAKING QUALITY PART OF THE PROCESS

Safety is Quality
Right away, it is appropriate to state "Safety Is Quality!" Any injury is a non-quality event that occurred in the execution of the work. Non-quality costs money. Injuries cost money; more than most executives dare to realize. Of course anyone can see the medical attention given an injured employee costs money.

As stated earlier, even more costly are all the indirect costs that accrue after an injury occurs. Lost time, lost productivity, poor publicity, are but three. Research accomplished by The Construction Industry Institute found that indirect costs run twice to twenty times the direct costs. In such a scenario an injury that has a medical/indemnity cost of $40,000 would have an indirect cost no less than $80,000, ranging to $800,000 when a lawsuit results. So having an injury free work culture is a profit protecting initiative. Therefore, employee safety is a quality issue of the first order.

The quality revolution may well be the single most significant development in American industry since the creation of the assembly line. Quality. What is it? Where can I find it? What can I do to get it? Where do I start? How do I measure it? How do I know if I have it? How do I keep it?

All are questions of the day. And so it should be. For too many decades American industry has failed to fully understand the defeating nature of a work place psychology of production first; quality, well yes, but not first. In the 1970's it seems that the entire production thrust of the United States that reached gigantic proportions became lost in the rough seas of consumer malcontent. Consumers found the product they sought was manufactured in another country, looked better, fit together better and worked better. The result was inevitable. In the 1990's American producers fought back. Juran, Deming and Crosby are now almost "household names." Where then does this need to embrace quality fit into our safety management system?

Embrace Standards of Quality
If you are following the "pathway to Zero Injury" then you must embrace quality concepts in your safety operations. First let me ask this question using Crosby's "right the first time" logic.

Have you ever engaged happily or contentedly in turning out a product that you knew full well would have to be redone when finished because you accepted that it would take you two or three times to get it right? Another example, more personal; you go for surgery. Ready for three efforts before reaching success? Or even two? NO! NO! Get a surgeon that will do it right the first time.

All of us, throughout our working lives have a single, common desire by nature of our implied job charter. "Let me do this. And do it right the first time." Some students of "quality concepts" who work in research or exploratory fields where trial and error may well be accepted have difficulty accepting "do it right the first time" as a valid concept. In such cases I believe those working in these activities need to focus on the experimental process asking such questions as, "Am I performing this effort in the right way every time?" Newly discovered inventions often see several stages of development before they are ready for service.

I think of "safety quality" in the following manner. Quality, in a sense, is the "fiber-optic" thread along which we design our path of safety progress in the tightly woven fabric of our integrated safety management system. Quality is the essence of our everyday safety effort. All safety programs, goals programs, review processes, people involvement effort, role definition, and conflict resolution; are aimed along this fiber-optic path. The "path of do it once so the problem goes away forever!"

Yes, we need to accept "quality concepts" into our safety management system. We must make it a part of the safety guidelines, goals, roles, procedures and reviews. We must build it in. After all, "a quality safety product" is the sought after result and will become the strength of your enterprise.

STEP TEN –

INVOKING PROGRESS NOW!

Progress Begins When You Begin

The author is the first to admit the safety management strategy advocated in the "integrated safety management system" approach is a significant departure from past practice by many line managers. As such, the approach will breed doubt in the minds of some who read this work. But if you fall into the category of the "tool box" safety manager and have tried them all, then what can you lose?

The biggest mental deterrent you may face in deciding to try this system will be "but I need progress now! Not later."

Let me assure you, safety results will begin just as soon as you begin. The "word" will fly through your organization. "Employee involvement" has an immediate productive "ring" to it. However, if you fail to follow through, your organization will suffer more than with any other of the "efforts" you have implemented in the past. The disappointment factor in being promised "employee involvement," only to see the boss fail to fulfill his word, will produce a significant negative morale result.

Safety progress will begin as soon as your people begin the goal setting process. Progress will begin when they begin to "think" about their goals. As the goals form in their minds, progress begins. Once it begins, and you follow through with the entire system, you will be on your way.

In recent years, the author has encountered managers responsible for safety, who at a given point in time, were experiencing rapid progress in reducing injury. On inquiry, it was found that sure enough, a tool was being used that highlighted "employee involvement" with parallel support from the top to commit resources to solve problems. Almost without exception, however, the managers so blessed were very concerned about what to do next. They had not yet realized that there within their grasp was the most powerful safety management process available. All they had to do was push the automatic button by taking the steps to implement the employee involved system of "tops down guidelines, bottoms up goals" on an annual basis with quarterly reviews.

Bottom-up Implementation Goals

Immediate progress is inevitable if you adopt a "bottom up" goals activity in the lower reaches of your organization. Using the Philip Crosby "quality is free" concept to fuel your "bottom up" goals thrust will insure the goals process will have problems to solve that yield an immediate safety return.

Releasing accountability, or control of your safety operations, is not advocated. The leader must always set the performance expectation, stay close to the action and "guide" it through quarterly safety goal reviews.

The typical authoritative managers do not "guide" his/her organizations; they "command" them. Do this, do that, all from the top. This "command psychology" will occur even if the manager does not intend to appear this way. Our American culture, to a large degree, dictates how people see the boss. And our cultural heritage has been authority and command!

"Guiding" is a much more delicate approach. Publish the "guidelines" which will set the tone, deal openly with the problems faced, ask for help and give your people the "format" for the "bottom up" help process.

A typical scenario, in the competitive business world of today, is that the top manager instinctively senses he needs help from the bottom. He asks for it only to see significant moral support from the organization produce little, if anything, of lasting consequence. Why?

The answer is because there is no system in place to allow the moral support to take on substantive form. The installation of the "integrated safety management system" is mandatory if you want safety progress on an evergreen basis.

<u>Use the Ten Steps</u>
Repeated: the ten Steps to form the "evergreen progress safety management system."
1. Setting the Safety Foundation
2. Getting Help for your Safety Culture Change
3. Using the Safety Team Help Process
4. Creating Safety Action Goals
5. Using System Operational Guidelines
6. Using the Safety Goals Review Process
7. Capturing the Progress
8. Working Out Relationships
9. Making Quality Part of the Process
10. Invoking Progress Now!

Customize it for your organization and you too will be amazed at the progress your people make in a very short time.

Chapter 17 - Safety Teams

Employee Involvement

<u>Elementary Safety Teams</u>
Each employer will need to examine the organization to determine just how the Safety Teams will need to be structured to insure the people on each team are interdependent. For instance, in the construction business, where there is typically high employee turnover, the Safety Team of choice can be the elementary type. "Elementary" simply means that the training of members is limited to being informed that they are part of an inter-connected safety team goal setting process. Of course, the foreman (leader) of each team will need instruction on how to function as a team leader. For the members, the role of their team and their individual role as team members is explained.

Elementary Safety Teams for projects or construction divisions are interconnected through the supervisory staff. A "bottom-up" goals scenario begins with the first level of supervision and progresses up the organization with each leader of a lower team being a member of the next level team. The foreman and the crew are the first team. The second level supervisor (Superintendent?) and the foremen reporting to him/her are the second level team, etc.

In basic fashion, the process begins with each team leader receiving a copy of the safety goals guidelines letter. The foremen start the "bottom-up" process by involving their crews in setting their safety technique implementation goals and activities. The subject areas for a foreman and crew are limited to those areas of safety where they are in ultimate control of the activities required to implement the goals the team sets. All other activities flow along the customary lines of authority for planning and execution.

Creating More Sophisticated Long Term Teams

There are many sources of help on how to set up a long-term sophisticated team concept. It is not a simple subject, nor can it be done quickly. To the contrary, much thought must be given to the how, who and what questions.

The how. How do I do it? Here I strongly urge you get an education in the use of the "team" management tool and how it can be applied to safety. Such will help answer the next two questions.

The who. Who should be on the safety team or teams?

The what. What do the safety teams work on? What is appropriate subject matter for their agenda? On what frequency should their meetings held?

Teams are a very powerful "Help Process." Safety Teams are organizational structure tools. These teams also need tools to use, tools with which they can address the appropriate subject matter, in the appropriate manner. They will need to learn how to manage their team meetings to make them effective.

Safety Team Authority

It is a common question when Safety Teams are established that the team members are unsure exactly what their scope of authority includes. This is an important subject and requires certain definition in order to reduce the non-productive time teams can spend discussing changes in areas outside their own scope of authority. See appendix on "What a team is and Is not."

Conflict out of Teams

When you activate the "Help Process" using "safety teams,"

one important asset that flows from these group meetings is the "divergent views" of the members. If you are the leader of your facility, it is important that you "highlight" your expectation that this difference of opinion will exist from time to time and that you urge all views be added to the discussions that the safety teams have as they work to reach consensus.

In a regular, ordinary authoritarian organization, this safety management process and these "divergent views" more commonly surface as "conflict." The safety team members will need training in how to productively deal with the conflict so that conflict becomes a "strength," rather than a weakness. Conflict can be a "weakness" if there is no recognition that it is, first of all, okay to have a different view, and second, that the safety team has been taught how to deal with conflict, and to work out differences to produce the "best" solution.

Compromise is not what is meant. Frequently compromise is worse than either expressed view in a conflict. But what is derived out of this conflict is that the best parts of the conflicting views are brought together in a consensus where all agree that the team has reached the soundest decision on a safety issue.

In surfacing conflict in the work place, typically one finds that conflict seems to arise over who is supposed to do what. Such conflict points to an understanding of roles problem. Defining roles will frequently yield astonishing progress in work efficiency. This has been found to be a result of the productive redirection of energy previously spent in irresolvable role conflict situations.

Safety Role Definitions
Who is responsible to insure that safety roles are developed? Those who lead must necessarily take the lead. Written

safety roles contain expectations. Those who are led need to know from their leaders who is expected to do what. Where does my role on this subject, issue or problem stop and who do I pass the action to? Does this person know that the next action step belongs to them because they, like I, understand the roles?

I cannot emphasize too strongly the importance of safety role development. Most assuredly safety role definitions will prove to be a significant productivity improvement item.

Be very careful not to imply that safety role definitions are all inclusive. Understanding should be clear that role definitions do not contemplate complete job definition but cover the principle items only.

Where do I start with role development? What departments should I do first? Both are frequently asked questions.

There are three basic approaches to making such a decision. One is to start where the activity is highest and is most subject to short-notice changes that alter the workflow. This will be an especially lucrative starting place if many different people need to react to those changes.

The second is to listen for evidence of conflict. Where conflict exists there is most always an "understanding of roles" problem. Occasional conflict will arise from personality differences and we'll deal with these under "Working out Relationships" later.

The third is to determine the process by mapping or flow charting and then use this product as the sharing document as you "talk out roles."

An important area in which to work out relationships for the safety team is to develop an understanding of the philosophical and real differences in the role of a Team

Leader (the boss) and the team members. It will be different than just a "boss." Being a "safety team leader boss" is much harder.

First, the role statements must make it very clear that line managers, supervisors and foremen are in charge of workplace safety. They are supervising the work and the work process, thus they are also in charge of a safe work process and a safe result free of injury. Safety Staff are placed in an organization as skilled advisors, sometimes inspectors and auditors and frequently safety trainers. Safety Staff are, via safety training, inspections and audits, your in house safety compliance personnel.

Safety personnel must never become safety rule enforcers in a Zero Injury Culture. One cannot EVER punish one's way to Zero Injury. HOWEVER, neither can one tolerate continued safety non-compliance from any employee. Action must always be taken to assist non-performers into a mind-set of commitment. This is equally true of the management staff as it is the other employees.

Management staff should view themselves living in a "glass house." As such they must expect any move or statement they make to be seen and interpreted as a measure of their individual safety commitment. In a Zero Injury Culture ALL management MUST buy-in, period. And must reflect that buy-in without fail. Just as care must be given by managers regarding their spoken words, likewise, for a leader to omit verbal support of safety during a meeting is also a serious omission. If you are a manager and you "forget" during an opportunity to "speak out in support" of safety, then you need to re-examine your level of commitment to a zero injury safety culture.

Chapter 18 - Managing the System

Avoid Temptation
There may be a temptation to shortcut what you have just read. My advice is to be careful. This is a proven system. Experience has shown that each Step of the system is vitally important to the health of the whole approach.

To be sure, as you manage the system after it has been installed, you will find it necessary to continually fine-tune each Step. New people will need to be "brought up to speed" and there is a very effective way to do this.

First explain the system and then let them become involved where appropriate; on teams, in the goals process, in the reviews. Recognize and accept that the reviews take time. It is very important to let those who were involved in establishing the goals to be a part of the progress reporting process and attend the goal review meetings with their supervisor and you.

Three benefits accrue. One, as leader you see each individual first hand and get a feel for their capabilities and potential; two, they can be a part of the presentation and thus they become much more committed, and three, they can hear your comments, concerns, and philosophy on a first hand basis. This gives them a sense of directed purpose without being autocratic.

In the bottom-up Goals process review, the Bosses' questions can easily become a part of the goal effort automatically due to the high interest level and buy-in to the bottom-up process. Care must be taken not to let your questions become unintended high priority goals. This tendency stems from a very basic fact. Committed people want to please! When you see the system working this way, "automatic progress" is being made. Another way to view this "automatic" phenomenon is, you now no longer have to ask someone to take on another challenge. You now need only to ask a question for goal clarification and any perceived added potential for progress is willingly added to the goal. And, just as importantly, if they are aware of problems they face that you did not perceive they will also willingly tell you about these.

Why? Because these are their goals! They own them and as they review them with you they are asking for your buy-in to their goals during the review process.

Management Attitude
The attitude of Top Management is the single most important ingredient above all others that will contribute to the success of your "integrated management system".

First, support for the system must emanate from the top. Management's enthusiasm, dedication, along with your visible support, must pervade the management cadre as an expected norm.

Second, in a sense, Top Management will be living in a glass house. All eyes will be focused on these leaders; testing the resolve, checking for example. Questioning; "Do I see action that correlates with what I am hearing?"

<u>You must pass this test!</u>

Third, having worked through the steps, you will begin to experience the growth of satisfaction in your own mind as the "integrated management system" begins to work.

How to Make Changes
Every manager should realize that even though you develop

this management system for automatic progress, on a random but regular basis events will occur that will create diversions. The need for additional goals that are short term and immediate will exist from time to time. Take these challenging events in stride. Fold them right into the management process. Priorities will have to change to accommodate the new goals but after all, the short-term need cannot be ignored.

On the longer time frame try with all your energy not to shock the long-term progress your system will afford you. If at all possible deal with the next needed changes in the work place during the next guidelines issue. This avoids diverting the energy that is on the verge of making that yet unseen step of progress.

So, you must be very careful in making any midstream changes in the guidelines. Direct the system as you would a symphony orchestra because in a sense you will be the orchestra leader and to change the score in the middle of the performance could easily destroy the quality of the finished product. Make your decision now that you want planned progress and realize to divert plans that are in place endangers all the work that has been done and serves to frustrate the people and the process. Decide now to consciously stand back and see dramatically reduced injury rates arrive!

PART 3

THE APPENDIX

The Zero Injury Guide Book

APPENDIX EXPLANATION

This appendix is provided to allow in-depth analysis of four important subjects the author considers salient to achieving a Zero Injury working culture.

Item 1. Articles on the "Sophisticated Safety Team Approach"

The following articles are most suitable for a employment situation where the employees are in place for a five year to career length term. This does not mean that Safety Teams are not effective for shorter terms. For shorter-term employment situations the teams will not need to go to the depth of sophistication the articles contemplate. These articles are titled:

A. Team Management - What it is. What it is not.
B. Conflict and Team Management
C. Team Decisions, Roles and Authority
D. "Openness and Trust" in Team Management

Team management is nothing new. Some leaders manage with teams without calling the process by that name. There are very sophisticated teams but "straight out of the box" teams are more abundant. These are very basic in their approach and for the purpose of obtaining safety management participation do not need a very high degree of sophistication.

If you wish to polish your safety teams to a high luster of professionalism then the following articles will assist that process.

The appendix includes four articles that were written "along the way" during the installation of the proven management system described in the book. They are written in the "here and now" time frame and had the common objective of helping the teams and people involved deal with some of the important interpersonal issues as they faced them.

These articles are offered in their original form and deal more with the function of a team in a general sense than just solely in the safety sense. They are for your reference and use as you set out to install "The System."

Item 2. The article on Monetary Incentives
E. Treatise on Monetary Incentives
There are many companies who do use the monetary incentive motivational approach to rewarding employees for achieving a zero injury workplace. Caution has been mentioned above, yet there are a number of employers that routinely give monetary incentive awards. What might be the logic in support of these actions. Presented below in this section is an analysis of this body of logic.

Item 3. The Zero Injury Safety Techniques
F. The CII Zero Injury Safety Incentives Explained
The nine critical Zero Injury techniques are explained in this section of the appendix.

Item 4. Return on Investment for Zero Injury
G. Details on how to construct an ROI Spreadsheet.

Item 1 - The Sophisticated Team Management Approach

A. TEAM MANAGEMENT. WHAT IT IS. WHAT IT IS NOT.

Business Decisions
A business and the environment in which it exists is constantly changing. This change is caused by outside forces as well as forces from within and requires business decisions to be made in response. How well these decisions are made determines the current and future health of the business.

Research has shown that where practicable, decisions reached using a participative management style, where all information bearing on the problem is shared by those affected, are typically more sound decisions than those reached using other management styles. Or saying it in a slightly different way -that all the interdependent individuals, pooling all their knowledge as a Team, can reach a better decision than any single member working alone.

Managers installing team management need to make it clear that participation is wanted. A team member must understand that in accepting the role of involvement in the decision making discussion there is a trade off being made. For the right to participate one vows to support the decision reached even though it may not go their way. This vow is in exchange for the opportunity to speak and participate and to contribute to and influence the decision making process.

When the members of a Team in a well-understood team process reach a decision, it is referred to as a "consensus" decision.

Team Management purpose is to reach the most sound

business decision possible. The process provides for –
1. Subject understanding
2. Open communications
3. The development of trust
4. The welcoming of ideas
5. Sincerely considering all opinions

Thus, it is a "participative" management style that gives opportunity for involvement.

We must recognize that people differ in their opinions regarding most any subject one can name. It is this difference that generally ensures that all sides of a question are discussed. As a group discusses a topic with each advancing a view and presenting the related logic, a "body of opinion" forms where most of the group members are in "general agreement". It is at this point that the members representing the minority view have then to take a commitment to the group that they will support the decision completely, even though they differ. It is then that a consensus decision is reached.

Without this individual commitment, the "openness and trust" advantage of the team style is lost when decisions become subverted by dissenting team members. One may as well then forget "team" management and use the "authoritarian" style where views are not solicited. For emphasis, we say again that one exchanges the "secret dissenting" posture that frequently results when authoritarian management style is used for a chance to be heard and offer input to decisions. Thus one gives support to the team decision even on those decisions where the consensus may not totally agree with one's personal view.

Are Teams New?
In William G. Dyer's book, "Team Building: Issues and Alternatives", the first chapter is entitled: "Teams are

everywhere." This is true. In reacting to the word "Team", we frequently think of sports. However, the Team concept applies to any group that has in common a "unity of purpose". This can be a chamber of commerce, a club, a family, church or employees in a business where customer service is the objective. In this latter case, a restaurant is an example where all the employees have the single objective to serve an enjoyable meal to the customer. Including clean dishes, a well-set table, appetizingly prepared food and cheerful table service.

Likewise, as employees in individual functions or services, we work with our fellow employee to accomplish a given task. This task can be to operate a unit, to maintain equipment, to test products for quality, to provide materials, to provide advice, to keep track of costs, and the list goes on and on. All of us, by the nature of our work, are associated in some way with a group of employees who have "unity of purpose".

Actually, all people working in a facility have a "unity of purpose" which is to manufacture products. Using possessive pronouns it would sound as follows:

"Our facility is ours to operate. Our Facility Team has this job to do. How well we do it depends very largely on how we relate to one another. If we relate poorly, we will not do a good job."

"The management style used here is one of the factors that determines how we relate to one another."

"It goes without saying, the problems are many that face us each day. How we approach these problems, how people work together in seeking solutions, reflects throughout the organization. If people work together and communicate well, the problems are understood and out on the table where we can see them and work on them; and we can move ahead. It is then, and only then, that a working climate can exist where all have a sense of worth and accomplishment. We can go home after our shift, or our day in the office, feeling that "today we got something done".

An Open Management Style
This "sense of worth and accomplishment" that we all like to have in the work place is enhanced by an open management style. Some call it a management style of involvement where each can speak their own opinion. Where all can be heard and each opinion does not fall on deaf ears; where each can call it like one sees it without fear, and where each can express their opinion freely in an honest and sincere way.

We need to recognize that with traditional management styles such an "all involved" working atmosphere has and can exist. This is especially so, where the leader of a group has a strong natural tendency toward the involvement style. There have been occasions where the leader invited all members of the group to a meeting and, in effect, a team session was held on a given problem.

Yet there is a distinct difference between a traditional management style and team style. Under most traditional systems, a leader works with group members as individuals. The most meaningful relationships exist between the leader and individuals. There is only limited interaction among the group as a whole. As a result, under traditional systems there is frequently a competitive relationship among the interdependent people needed to accomplish the task.

Team management reduces the non-productive competition among individuals working toward a common task. It brings these individuals together simultaneously with the leader and helps them understand each other. The result is an increased appreciation by the individuals, one for the other. This builds an environment of mutual trust, cooperation, and support, which allows better decisions to be made through the Teams. Are there other uses for Teams? Yes, once teams are in place and meeting regularly, these meetings also provide excellent means to discuss and understand a wide range of subjects. They also offer opportunity to pass information through the organization. Thus, there is a considerable improvement in information flow and in the consistency of understanding.

However, team management, to be effective as a style, has to be the style people want. One cannot force a Team relationship to exist where one is not wanted. Sure, the team members can be designated, but this does not create a relationship of "openness and trust" that comes with mature team development. This is true at any management level in the organization. It takes cooperation one with another to have an open management style.

The act of "management" starts with each employee. Each manages their contribution each day. Employees in the facility using their skills are in charge of and manage their contributions. A foreman, supervisor, manager, superintendent, or general manager is similar in this regard to a secretary, a clerk, an analyst, a draftsman, or an engineer.

Team Decisions - When?
A frequently asked question is "What kind of decisions can a "team" make? If I assist in decision making does this mean as a team member I have more authority? Let's explore situations where a "Team is and is not" needed to reach a decision. Take the example of a car pool and say a group of people get together and agree to share rides to work. As a "car pool team" they can discuss freely and seek agreement on: 1) what the driving rotation order will be, 2) what time they will leave the homes or work, 3) what route they will take, 4) how fast they drive, or 5) whether or not they will stop to have

coffee or eat. All these subjects can be "teamed" because there is "unity of purpose" and all can contribute.

But if on the day you are driving to work, an eighteen-wheeler approaches head-on in your lane you won't need a team decision to hit the ditch. Similarly, if "X" wants unleaded gasoline in his car, that's not a Team decision. Of if "Y" wants to use his own car rather than his wife's, that may be her decision and she is not on the car pool team.

So, one of the challenges in defining and using Team Management is that of understanding what is appropriate subject matter for a Team. Basically, it is much easier to "make team decisions" on longer range problems and procedures than those with immediate decision needs; i.e., the Eighteen Wheeler problem.

On the other hand, if the car pool team mentioned can get "Y" to agree to take up the subject of his wife's car with his "Family Team," then one Team can access another Team through the common member concept. "Y" is a member of the "Pool" Team and "Y's" own "Family Team". Also illustrated is that even though "Y" is on two different Teams, "Y" does not have more authority. However, the atmosphere does exist allowing "Y" to participate.

Similarly, in a team management environment it can be true that the leader of one Team is also a member of another Team. This allows communications up and down and across the organization to flow more rapidly, more smoothly and more effectively. With such a team management culture one can surface concerns, long held, because an effective means to be heard did not exist.

We must recognize the distinctiveness of a team environment; it is where new ideas are encouraged and frank expression of views are not only allowed but wanted. Team meetings are the opportunities to air these views and ideas. As this team effort goes forward, also recognize that the day-to-day routine execution of work and the normal mode of overview and instruction given by supervision will continue to function. Altering the style of decision making to where certain selected problems are solved by a team does not change the fact that each still must manage their contribution and area of responsibility.

Team Relationships
One of the challenges is that of building this Team relationship. Successful Teams do not just "happen," the atmosphere of "openness and trust" must be mutually sought by all members. To do this, special Team Building meetings are helpful. These meetings are usually called "workshops" and are a day or two in length. Relationship techniques can be used by a facilitator to assist the Team develop as an effective work group.

A successful Team is very much dependent upon the leadership technique the leader uses. The leader must be willing to share some of the decision-making that he/she has control over with the Team. The key word here is "some" of the decisions. This does not mean "all the decisions" a leader must make can be put to the team. The leader decides which and when.

In this regard, the leader must not bring a subject to the Team for a decision unless the leader is completely committed to the concept of abiding by and living with the decision the Team reaches.

Further, the leader should not bring to the Team a problem where a decision has been reached at a higher management level and offer the problem "as a decision open for consensus" resolution. In such a case, however, the leader may be willing to give the Team the latitude to decide how to implement such a previous higher-level decision. The leader, therefore, has the important responsibility to identify these problems to the Team in a way that lets the Team know the decision constraints.

In a team meeting where a team decision is wanted, a leader must use care not to "bull-doze" personal ideas across. The leader's challenge is to maintain a role as a team member on an equal level with other team members while the various aspects of the topic are being discussed. The leader's role is critical in setting the climate so that the team can effectively reach a consensus decision on a subject that the Team is to decide.

Otherwise, team meetings will merely consist of the team leader manipulating the team members to accept the leader's own strongly held views.

Team Management - What It Is - Is Not
Let's examine what "Team Management is, and what it is not" to a team member.

Team Management -
is not - a way for each of us to get what we individually and sometimes perhaps selfishly "want" accomplished.

is - a way for each of us to get what we individually want communicated to others. Also, to the degree that we can get others, through this communication technique, to agree; then, yes it is a way to accomplish what we want.

Team Management -
is not - a style that yields permissiveness. The fact that a leader uses the team style does not remove the leader's authority or accountability for the results.

is - how a team member, at the appropriate time, can raise an idea or issue regarding a rule, policy, or procedure and participate in the discussion. And "if" the team leader has delegated this particular area to the team, then a decision may be by the team.

Team Management -
is not - the way to accomplish the urgent, immediate task. In these cases, we seek quick advice as needed and move rapidly.

is - the method to get a procedure established that defines the way we make a decision in a particular urgent matter the next time it comes up. In such cases what the team is doing is this; if a particular identified event occurs in a sudden and urgent manner then the action taken will be thus, as pre-decided by the team.

Team Management -
is not - a style that ensures that every individual will be involved in every decision reached.

is - the way that the appropriate individuals are included in the decision process at the appropriate working level.

Team Management -
is not - where a group of people get together and take a vote to reach a decision.

is - where a group works to reach a consensus through a thorough discussion of all points and where all members voice their views; where difference in ideas are highlighted with the group seeks to take the best parts of all the ideas, putting them together to reach a better decision.

Team Management. Will it work?
The answer depends on our willingness to -

- Develop a personal attitude of openness and trust.
- Analyze what is appropriate for our Team to handle.
- Communicate our views in a style that does not criticize other approaches.
- Live with and support the Team decision even though at times it does not agree with one's own preference.

The team management approach is used to increase participation. There are many areas where experience will help the learning process. The challenge is to think through each step very thoroughly to insure that each step taken is one that is positive. As progress is made forums need to be developed that allow individuals to share experiences with others. This allows a more rapid build in total experience base.

B. CONFLICT AND TEAM MANAGEMENT

Recognizing Conflict
The news media of today typically uses the word conflict to reflect that a war is being fought or a battle is raging. For this reason, we sometimes hesitate to use the word conflict in a "Team Management" environment. Rather, we may say, "Why, we are a Team. Team Management means we have good relationships, we pull together to get the job done, and we seldom, if ever, have an argument. What do you mean conflict? That's a bad word around here!"

Yes and no!

Yes, we usually maintain good relationships, and yes we get the job done.

No, conflict is not a bad word around here.

The following pages will explain why "conflict" is not a bad word around here.

First, let's define "conflict" for our purposes in the management process. "Conflict" is simply a way to say "we are in disagreement. We do not see eye to eye. Our opinions differ on the issue."

Up front, let's set the record straight. "The better decisions are often born out of this reality of divergent views that we call conflict." Therefore, we need to learn how to deal with conflict and obtain the benefit from it.

Conflict resolution between party "A" and party "B" is one of four things. A wins B to their position, B wins A to their position or A and B each build on the ideas of the other to change a bit reaching a common position. Or after discussion, A and B find that the perceived difference did not exist. Research has shown that in solving a complex problem, two or more people (not to exceed a practical working size) putting their knowledge together using a productive process with a willingness to participate in give and take will usually reach more sound decisions than any one of the participants acting alone.

Many business firms go to great lengths to hire the brightest, most innovative, and inventive people possible. It is people with ideas and with the ability to put their ideas to work in creative ways that yields progress. These people are typically somewhat aggressive. They are known as "doers". Let it be understood that one should not in any way diffuse this potential. Indeed, the opposite is true. It is this participative team management environment that insures that this potential for creativity has a chance to surface and we can capitalize on this asset called conflict.

Our Values Examined
Okay then, with conflict out of the "closet", so to speak, let's think a bit about our personal behavior, attitude and "moldability" as we go through the process to resolve conflict. To some degree, this conflict we have comes out of differences in values from one individual to the next. These values are part of us. As we deal with conflict, we knowingly and sometimes unknowingly apply these personal values as we present our views and as we consider the views of others. Values come in different categories. Some of them could be categorized as follows:
- Moral
- Social
- Cultural

Some of our values are related to lessons we have learned during our lives that "taught" us how we feel and what we feel about certain aspects of living, working, managing, and interrelating with others. Our ability to "trust" others can be placed in this group if we recognize that moral, social, and cultural values also affect this "trusting" that we do.

There is, however, another source of values called "situation values". Sometimes our "situation" is referred to as "climate" or "environment" to describe our work "situation". If we set out to create a work situation that is enjoyable, we try to create an enjoyable atmosphere where people are friendly, courteous, and helpful.

Where we "value" these things we create such a place to work and then being friendly, courteous, and helpful become "situation values."

Right away, let's say we do not claim this list of "values" is necessarily complete. What we are saying is that this effort to list values, we feel, will lead us to better understand the reasons for conflict.

Our Judgments
Our judgments as individuals are based on our values, which on any given subject, will be fairly complex in the way the values are interwoven into the fabric of our opinion. If we are realistic, we must recognize that a really tough type of conflict that occasionally occurs is the basic "personality conflict." Such situations can be described as when two people due to personal traits that so annoy one another that they are unable of their own power to overcome their basic dislike for each other. It's sad but true.

It's also true that if we strive mightily, most of these can be overcome. Those that can't, must be recognized and the parties need to understand that in the final analysis our jobs do require these parties to work constructively together to accomplish mutually dependent tasks. While liking one another is nice and desirable in the work place, it is not mandatory. But I must say this; If general, wide-spread "dislike," one for the other, is pervasive in the workplace the organization will struggle continually. I also believe such a workplace is a very remote possibility.

We need to maintain that moral values and convictions are very important. In the business world, we must stand on a sound moral base of honesty and integrity to be successful in the long term.

Our Feelings
Added to the values we have, making them even more complex are our "feelings" about our values. Some of us wear our "feelings" up front, where we test what we hear or the actions we see and often react in a rapid, decisive, emotional way to what we see and hear. Usually, this type of reaction creates an instant issue. This kind of sensitivity is okay if we do not "turn off" the other party. It is important that we surface our "feelings" but try to be constructive in our response. A response that is so firm and unduly strong that it "turns off" the conflict process is not productive.

Usually, we will be working on conflict resolution where that conflict is based on opinion, feelings, and perceptions. And the parties must be sincere in their effort to arrive at the most sound decisions in the resolution of the issue. Also conflict frequently is caused by what one either "sees" or "hears" or in some cases what one "thinks" they see or hear. First, let's think about what we "see", then we'll deal with the problems arising out of what we "hear." In the realm of interpersonal relations where conflicts occur, the old adage still holds true that says:

"I can't hear what you're saying because of what I see you doing."

It's still said today that a parent who instructs a child to "do what I say, not what I do" is a very ineffective teacher.

If we accept this as truth, then it is easy to understand that for "conflict" to have a chance of being resolved, what we say and what we do must be in harmony. Nothing is more defeating and discouraging than to think you have "talked" out a conflict and feel that understanding now exists and then discover the other party is still "acting" in the same old manner.

Now let's deal with what we "hear". Equally important in our "conflict" resolution process is our world of words. Our vocabulary. We use words to express our ideas, concepts, and feelings. Our use of specific words can be the cause of an apparent conflict on an "idea" we are expressing. Not because of conflict in "ideas" between the two individuals, but rather because in the two minds there is a different meaning attached to a "word" that gets inserted into the conversation. All of us have no doubt in times past engaged in heated discussions arising from apparent conflict, only to discover that, as far as the real "issue" was concerned, we were not in disagreement at all and had suffered through the dialog due to personal differences in the meaning behind a specific word.

Our "Moldability"
As individuals, once we have what we say and what we do in harmony, then we can maintain awareness that there is the ever-present potential for ill-founded conflict to arise out of word usage. Our next challenge on the road to productive use of conflict is our "attitude" about the process. Our own "moldability", if you will. It is suggested that one of the secrets to getting the most out of the conflict resolution process is that of individual open-mindedness and personal "moldability". Moldability, in the sense that we as individuals are not suffering from a case of "tunnel vision." We are capable of seeing all sides of the issue. That we can indeed listen, hear, and understand from others all the factors they

feel bear on the decision and are willing to listen. Yes, and even be persuaded to move or "remold" our position as we gain knowledge from the input of others.

At this point, we may find some people who are personally so competitive that their personality cannot tolerate "giving in". These persons tend to be immovable and as such are not very moldable. Hence, they have a basic problem that will prevent them from playing a full role in a participative management environment where the value of the decisions reached through conflict resolution is encouraged.

Our Patience
Now, one last point that is perhaps one of the most important of all is our personal "patience;" patience with the resolution process and patience with others. Opinions and feelings formed over years aren't changed instantly. It takes an in-depth discussion of alternatives and the logic behind them. It takes time to resolve conflict to get that "better" end product.

Summary
In summary, healthy conflict is productive. If we can effectively resolve our conflict and thereby capture the opportunity for progress, then our already good relation-ships can improve and we can get the job done even better and have fun doing so. One of the unique strengths of a team management environment that is lacking in other management styles is the opportunity it provides to more fully capture the progress that can arise from conflict.

C. TEAM DECISIONS, ROLES AND AUTHORITY

Safety Team Leader Role
Team Management as a name, implies a participative management style. In our routine use of the word "Team" it also implies a group with a leader, captain, or coach. An industrial setting incorporates a work groups' traditional "boss" as the Leader of a group as it seeks to become a Team.

A safety team cannot function without the willing partici-pation of the Leader in the process. Actually, that is what participative management is all about: the Leader sharing his decision-making responsibilities with the group he supervises.

Borrowing from the above article "Team Management - What It is, What It Is Not", we find the following comment regarding the role of the Leader.

"A successful Team is very much dependent upon the technique the Leader uses. A willingness must exist on the part of the leader to share some of the decision making with the Team.

In this regard, the Leader must not bring a subject to the Team for a decision unless the Leader is completely committed to the concept of abiding by and living with the decision the Team reaches.

Further, a leader must not bring to the Team a problem where a decision has been reached at a higher management level and offer the problem as one open for consensus decision. In such a case, however, the Team may be given the latitude to decide how to implement such a previously made decision. The Leader, therefore, has the important responsibility to identify these problems to the Team in a way that lets the

Team know what the decision constraints are.

In a team meeting where a team decision is needed, a Leader must use care not to "bull-doze" personal ideas across. The challenge is to maintain a role as a team member on an equal level with other team members while topics are being discussed. The Leader's role is critical in setting the team climate so it can effectively reach consensus on items the Team is to decide."

Authority and Accountability

Let's examine then how one determines what are appropriate matters for a given Team to decide. It is obvious that to make a decision the Team needs the authority.

Authority, in corporations, is delegated down through the organization. Along with authority to decide, goes the additional concept of responsibility and accountability. These two concepts differ a bit from authority.

When a higher management level delegates "authority to decide," it has to release its right to make that decision. However, although higher management holds lower management responsible and accountable, it cannot thereby release its own share of the burden. Although shared by lower management levels, higher management remains responsible and accountable for any decisions made at lower levels in the organization.

It is the task of the Team Leader to decide the areas in which he has the decision authority and what decisions he will be willing to share with the Team.

Leader Sharing and Support

Remember, as teams are created, the decision process is moving from an authoritarian/consultative management style toward increased use of participative style. At each level, the leader is still responsible and accountable for satisfactory performance results in his area of supervision.

The leader will naturally have some apprehension about sharing the management role with the work group. As the leaders' confidence and trust in the work group as a decision-making team increase, an increasing amount of the decision-making will be delegated to the team.

There is a rather significant challenge facing the work group (Team) as well. As they find their Leader willing to share, the Team must realize that they are also responsible and accountable for the results of their decisions. The Team must, as individuals, be sensitive to the pressures that are on the Leader and give support and patience.

Likewise, the Leader must be alert to needs of the team members to be informed of the background information on issues that the Leader decides unilaterally or in consultation. Increased openness and trust are vital to increased use of the Team concept.

The Leader must learn how to share increasing amounts of information on decision issues with the Team. This will assist the Team in being understanding and patient toward the Leader.

A pitfall which some team members sometimes find themselves experiencing is the following: Typically, a team member feels increasing participation and opportunity to dialogue with the Team and Team Leader on many new subjects. As a result, the team member may tend to lose sight of their subordinate role and offer undue resistance when a Leader decides an issue without team input. At this point, the team style allows the subject to be raised and discussed at a team meeting, but it nevertheless remains the Leader's right to make the decision until willing to release the decision process on that issue to the team.

For instance, if on the issue of safety, a Team Leader felt the Team had insufficient aggressiveness in the pursuit of safety, the Leader may resort to consultative or authoritarian style in an attempt to raise the Teams' responsiveness to the situation. However, when one is looking for motivational techniques to deal with a subject like improving the Team aggressiveness in pursuit of safety, the Leader can use a combination of management styles.

The same (raising the Team's responsiveness to safety) task becomes more challenging if the person seeking improved aggressiveness in the pursuit of safety on the part of the team is a team member other than the Leader. In this latter case, the team member must use persuasive logic to win support from other team members for his position. In short, this member must do a "selling job". In such an example as this, the Team Leader faces the management challenge of openness in order to permit the interested team member to pursue this objective.

So one readily sees that the Team Leader sets the tone of team meetings, and through his "team leader" technique yields to the team in an appropriate fashion certain decisions. In all cases, it is the Team Leader's job to evaluate subject matter in order to assure the decisions that are made can be supported as sound alternatives. As a team matures in ability and understanding of its role, the Team can assist the Leader in this evaluation process.

D. THE CONCEPT OF "OPENNESS AND TRUST" IN TEAMS

Defining Openness and Trust

The words "openness and trust" are frequently used in discussing and understanding participative management. We hear them or see them and say to ourselves, "Oh yes, that's what we need alright. We need more Openness and Trust. I'll sure be happy when they tell me more and trust me more. That will sure improve how I feel about this place."

Wait. Let's not forget that openness and trust involves people. All people. For openness and trust to exist, the first step is to realize that it not only includes "they," it also cannot occur without "me." Each one of us must make our individual contributions for "openness and trust" to continue to develop.

To begin to understand the meaning of "openness and trust," let's deal with the word meanings separately and then bring them back together to see how they intertwine in concept.

Trust

Trust might be defined as the placing of confidence in another. Sounds simple. Why then do we not see more of it going on around us? Each of us can think of ways that we place confidence in others. One example is being acted out continuously on our highways, especially on those that are not divided highways. We drive our automobile in one direction at say 50 miles per hour while in the opposite direction a scant few feet away, a complete stranger does the same thing. We trust this stranger, and they us, to drive an automobile that is in safe condition in an alert and responsible manner.

A slightly different situation is experienced when one boards an airliner, or a bus or simply agrees to ride while another drives.

Thinking in this way we can literally think of thousands of illustrations of "trust" in our society.

If this much trust is going on within us and around us, why then suggest we would benefit from "more trust." These things we think of are examples of trust that are exhibited in physical ways. Another area in which we experience "trusting" is in the emotional, ideological, and personal information areas. These areas are "what we are," "who we are" and "how we feel."

Trusting others to perform in the illustrated physical way is somewhat easier than trusting another with information from our personal knowledge base about our work or about our selves. Especially so, if this is personal information which could damage us were it handled in an irresponsible and non-confidential fashion. The common question then is "Is it being suggested then that you want me to divulge more personal information? For what reason?" We reply, "That information is indeed personal, it is mine, mine alone and I do not want it known, you can forget it."

Right on! Divulging that personal information that you do not want known is not required in teams. We are talking primarily about sharing work related information in a more effective way.

So now we are into "divulging" information to someone we trust. Isn't that the same as "openness"? Yes it is and thus the first evidence of the inter-dependency of the words "openness and trust." But on with "trust."

Consider the following statement: "For me to trust you, I have to feel you are trustworthy. That if I become more open, you will handle that openness in a responsible fashion. That you will not joke around with that which is serious to me and that you will not use this bit of information against me, or to take advantage of me."

Developing Trust

Okay then, if that illustrates the "trust" we are talking about then how does one go about developing trust in relationships on the job?

First, we must communicate. Communicate, with each other, something of ourselves, our ideas, our concepts, in the areas of what we are. Both in terms of our job and related information and in terms of emotions, ideology and some amount of information that helps the other to see us better, to understand our motives.

Second, we must develop a willingness to accept that which we have learned about the other and at the same time also accept the person. Each person possesses a specific set of personal values. These values are measuring rods. We use them to evaluate situations, what we hear, see and yes, other people. In a sense "I am what I am" and "You are what you are" and "I accept you." "I may or may not agree, but I nonetheless accept you."

Third, along with being accepted by others we need to improve our ability to better understand ourselves by learning to look inward at what we really are. This does not at the same time imply that we are necessarily "happy" with ourselves. It may be that we may want to change a bit to be more effective in the area of human relationships. This change we may want to make can be in one or more of different specific ways. An example might be that one would want to develop their "listening" skills, or perhaps to be less "impulsive" etc.

Development of trust in relationships is not a rapid process. For instance we meet a person, we begin to talk at first about our hobbies, our families and about our feelings. It is at this "feelings" level that we begin to develop a understanding about this person and they us. The sharing has already begun, the opening of self ever so slightly has begun, always at first with those little things that are part of us, but that are easier to share and are more difficult to misuse. Then later, if the mutual interest allows and mutual respect builds, a bit more information of a slightly more risky nature is divulged and so on. This process is rarely a rapid one but usually takes considerable amounts of time.

This revealing of self will form a small segment of the typical information flow that is discussed in the workplace. The majority being the information we have as a function of our job. Included in this will be information that comes as part of our job objectives, our job role, our job authority and our personal information about our job.

This job related information bank is what we use to do our part in contributing to the work accomplishment process in our work place. Our communications to others from this information bank comes in both verbal and written forms. Sometimes it will be a decision that is directional in nature and we pass it on as "what must be done." Sometimes it will be simply a small segment of information that another person or group can use in their work process or decision making.

This information that we pass on is our individual contribution. Others see this information that we offer out of context with our personalities unless there is a mechanism and a willingness to let ourselves, our motives, our thinking, be known. As we develop "Openness" in this way, it relates to our work or job oriented information and then personal openness begins to have a direct impact on how effectively we work together in getting our work done.

Openness

Some people who are not naturally very open or trusting tend to share minimum amounts of information. They tend to have just enough openness to contribute to a decision but no more. Often background information that reveals the "why" behind the information offered will be omitted. In such cases the decision gets made but people do not understand why and have minimal sense of participation.

As we "open up" a little, higher levels of understanding are created where eventually a person can know the basic information behind a decision and understand it more fully. At this point perhaps an optimum level of knowledge exists and people feel informed and feel that they are contributing from a well-balanced knowledge base and have a feeling of importance in their job.

Participative or team management carries this "openness and trust" concept a step further. In appropriate situations the objective is to allow more of the decision making to drop to lower levels in the organization. Along with this decision making authority of course must flow all the necessary information from across the organization to the decision-making "Individual or Team."

With this information the deliberative process can begin. In a team discussion, each team member offers their own appropriate contribution, as a function of their knowledge base. Each team member strives to be trusting, communicative, and accepting of others in order for all members to have an identity with their personal values known and understood. This "openness and trust" then has a direct influence on the quality of the ultimate decision and each feels free to contribute.

Openness and Trust

"Openness and trust", two words intertwined inseparably in a participative work place contribute significantly to the creation of an effective working environment.

What does an organization gain from such development? The simple, but true hypothesis is that as we know one another better, appreciation for one another develops, anxieties and uncertainty are reduced, and the organization functions in a much improved fashion. Last, but not least, such an environment permits considerably more enjoyment to be realized as our work is performed.

Item 2 - Treatise on Monetary Incentives

The Arguments:

Monetary Safety Incentives for the worker?
Though I am reluctant to advocate the use of monetary incentives for reasons explained above on page 85 and 86, in order to be balanced in the treatment of incentives I am including this subject in the appendix.

Safety Awards versus Safety Incentives
It is important to differentiate between safety recognition awards and safety incentives. I cannot really say at what value an award becomes an incentive but the concept is that if an award gets large enough it becomes an incentive. Or if an award is known in advance it can become an incentive.

The opponents define an incentive as when the value of the item given exceeds the "monetary" cultural requirement to report all injuries and injury reporting isn't 100 percent. In other words, if the incentive is likely to cause under-reporting of injuries then at this point it becomes a deterrent rather than an incentive. There is logic to this argument.

The Vested Interest Concept
It is quite rational thinking to expect an individual to protect that in which a vested interest is held. In this regard, each of us works to keep alert so we protect our body against the pain and suffering caused by injury. Therefore, one can expect a worker to routinely do his or her job safely, avoiding injury to one's self, insofar as knowledge of danger and absence of a reckless nature will allow.

The instinct of "Self Protection" is obtained through personal experience and from the knowledge of others (teachers, trainers, instructors, supervisors and other colleagues) and their written materials. "Uncalled for risk taking" is usually brought under control through the same educational means, or on occasion perhaps an employer must resort to punishment to subdue a reckless nature.

Through safety education our "vested interest" level is empowered thus raised to where our "self preservation instinct" comes into sharper focus. We learn to think before we act, or as is the case many times, we learn to honor our thoughts more readily. Importantly safety training further equips the employees to be aware of "at-risk" behaviors the employer wants them to avoid.

The Paramount Question
Even so, a paramount question arises in worker attention to personal safety. "Can a worker's level of safety awareness, and thus their 'vested interest' and `self preservation' instinct be stimulated in a positive sense to higher than routinely normal levels?"

It is quite common to see or hear in the testimony of an injured worker the expression "I knew I shouldn't do that," or "I just wasn't thinking." Hearing these testimonies the question again arises. "Can one's self-preservation instinct and thinking be stimulated by means outside the individual to greater levels with the result being to raise to a higher level the instinct of self preservation?" And thus achieve a higher level of attention to "injury avoidance."

Safety Recognition Awards Are Used to Do This
Safety awards are recognized as tools used by employers to show appreciation for safety achievements. But do they increase worker attention to "injury avoidance?" Combinations of awards such as belt buckles, ball caps, tee shirts, jackets, decals, gift certificates, dinners, picnics, and other "things" have been used for many years. Many feel that these awards are useful in stimulating employees to work safer.

Some argue that while showing appreciation is very important and employees do feel good about it, recognition per se' does not stimulate an pronounced safer approach to work unless the award takes on a significant value such as a monetary incentive.

I wish to point out here that prior to making the decision to use monetary incentives there are important "first things first" considerations that an employer should note.

The Importance of a Safety Program
A well documented, publicized and worker understood "safety program" must always be the foundation on which safety incentive programs are managed. Once the employer has the "safety program" in place and safety orientation and training ongoing, what else can be done to further lower the occurrence of injury?

How Can Injuries Be Further Reduced?
How can a company's employees routinely achieve the level of "Zero Recordable" injuries. Can a worker's "self preservation" instinct be raised to higher levels through monetary incentives?

It seems to most employers that it is impossible to get beyond the continued occurrence of that "it should not have happened" injury." Yet, there are those who do achieve "Zero Recordable " injury.

The "Zero Injury" Achievers Are Increasing In Number!
Contractors who have embraced the notion that Zero Injury is a workplace value they want their companies to adopt have steadily increased over the past decade. These have implemented the research based results known as the Construction Industry Institute Zero Injury techniques.

Many have also utilized the Construction Industry Institute

Zero Injury Technique of monetary incentives. Some use this feature in conjunction with other awards of lesser value while others rely solely on the monetary incentive. These who do feel the incentive feature assists them reaching that illusive "Zero" injury level.

Some have tried monetary incentives without the CII Zero Injury Techniques only to find no success. As the research indicates, success still requires that most important ingredient of all, "skill in human relations" and use of the Zero Injury Techniques.

Selling employees on the concept of Zero Injury requires a sincerity of purpose and a "caring" that is recognizable by the employees. Employees then become co-advocates of a Zero Injury working culture the result being Zero Recordables for the life of the project or as a minimum, for very long periods of time.

The Incentive Feature
A "monetary incentive" is the feature: a "money per work-hour" bonus for Zero Injury safety excellence. It must be noted the proponents are reaching the achievement of "Zero" injury with increasing frequency. The incentive is paid in a separate check given to the worker by the foremen, or higher authority at the end of each lost time injury free pay period or at a minimum, monthly. The incentive is "always" for all and is based on the performance of all. All employees, including foremen, receive the bonus if there are "Zero recordable" injuries for the month. If any employee suffers an injury during the month no one receives the bonus. However, it is noted some employers give the incentive for a "Zero Lost Workday Case" frequency.

The Arguments Against
There are four recognized arguments against the use of monetary incentives. These are

a. "where does the bonus money come from?"
b. "why pay for self preservation?"
c. tempted to overuse "light duty" and
d. the working injured problem:

These questions are recognized as valid and will be dealt with further on.

The Performance Improvement
Many of those who have added the use of a "monetary incentive" along with the other CII Zero Injury Techniques are routinely achieving safety performance 10 to 20 times better than the national average. And many are achieving "Zero" Recordable injuries through the life of projects.

While saying the above it must be recognized that there are some contractors that are also achieving Zero Recordables that do not pay monetary safety incentives.

Why The Improvement with Incentives?
How and why is this happening? What can explain this injury free phenomenon? One can only conclude, after examining the evidence, that in these cases the worker is experiencing a heightened level of "self preservation" due to the increase in "vested interest" resulting from the "monetary incentive." With this an increased frequency of employee to employee safety communication is achieved.

Some argue without monetary incentives for all, it is not OK to warn a fellow worker. It is a "not my business" or "he knows what he is doing, so I'll just keep my mouth shut" situation. But now "my bonus check will go down the tube if you get hurt, so stop that unsafe act" becomes the talk of the day.

All employers should be cautious to insure all injuries are reported. Unreported injuries do not benefit the overall commitment to a zero injury working culture. Many feel, not so surprisingly, that injuries not reported, over time produces a culture where injury is not reported, producing an "imaginary safe working culture."

Relationships Are Important
The relationship among employees, and the relationship between employees and their supervision is a significant factor in safety performance. If, through common vested interest, one can open up these lines of communication so information flows more openly and freely, then a zero injury project is more easily achieved.

On the other hand, if employees do not get along well with each other and if employees hold their supervision in disdain, then the opportunity for zero injury to be achieved is severely impaired. As it always has been, "Success in safety excellence is highly dependent on mental attitude and mental attitude is dependent on relationships."

Incentive proponents argue that collectively awarded monetary incentives open up the channels of communication. And when employers care enough to give monetary incentives, the supervision (also getting the same incentive) are motivated to keep the communications open by treating the employees with an increased level of concern. They all have a common "vested interest" in achieving a no injury jobsite. The "self preservation" instinct is increased and the quality performance level of Zero Injury is more easily achieved.

Back to the Arguments Against
Let's now go back to the arguments against the "safety incentive bonus" approach and take them one at a time, last first. A. Where does the safety bonus money come from?, B. Why pay for self-preservation?, C. Tempted to overuse light duty, And , D. The working injured problem.

The Zero Injury Guide Book

The Working Injured
The working injured concern results from the temptation of a worker to hide an injury and continue to work with possible aggravation of the original injury. This is a real issue and in a monetary incentive environment steps must be taken by the employer to insure that this does not occur. It is a fact that employees have been known to hide injuries because they did not want their colleagues to lose their safety incentive. OSHA often looks skeptically at monetary incentive programs if they are administered in absence of any real substantive effort to create a Zero Injury culture.

We all know that occasional cases of non-reporting of injuries occur on all projects. Monetary incentive opponents believe incentives increases the chance of this occurring. But, proponents say to use this reason as a principal argument against safety incentive payments may be to say, that eliminating the human suffering of work place injury to at, or near, zero injury through improved safety communication is not worth taking the chance that a few employees may aggravate or not report a hidden injury.

Overuse of Light-Duty Work
Proponents believe light-duty work properly assigned can be equally productive to any other work. Non-legitimate use of light duty-work is not appropriate in a Zero Injury management effort. With reduced injury frequency will come a reduction in the need for light-duty assignments. If a company's or project's light-duty policy is seen by the workers as a sham then likely light-duty is being overused or at a minimum miss-used.

Paying For Self-Preservation
Proponents argue that a safety bonus is but a "productivity payment." In this sense it is no different than the base wage. Worker productivity is exchanged for base wage. Separating

safety performance, an easily measured metric and productivity item, from the base wage concept and using a bonus for zero injury achievement is as sound a concept as base wage they argue.

Where does the incentive money come from?

The money we are talking about is now being spent now for injury! The direct and indirect cost of worker injury is much higher than most people realize. Though some of the cost is at the expense of the injured worker; i.e., reduced wages and the inconvenience of injury, the larger share of the cost falls on the employer. Injury costs are much higher than prevention costs!

Research has shown that the indirect costs exceed the direct costs (those costs covered by Workers' Compensation insurance) by a factor of 2 to 20 to one. Just looking at base Workers' Compensation premium alone one finds the cost of construction worker injury as determined by the premiums paid for insurance ranging from $1.00 to over $5.00 per hour across the 50 states with the national average being around $2.50 per work hour.

Simply adding the indirect costs in at a 1 to 1 ratio doubles these losses to $2.00 and $10.00 per work hour with the average being $5.00 per hour. These costs are not just for work hours lost but are for all hours worked by construction employees! This national average cost equates to an Injury Cost of over $1,000,000 per 100 construction employees.

With 7,000,000 construction employees in the USA, this national cost of injury for the construction industry of (7,000,000/100) x 1,000,000 =
   $70,000,000,000 (Seventy Billion Dollars per year).

Reducing injury in a company to levels of near zero saves a large amount of money that historically has reduced an employer's ability to compete and has directly reduced profit margin. Proponents of monetary incentives believe that sharing a portion of the savings accruing as a result of safe work with the safe worker will create a "common vested interest" climate. The employees get an incentive and the employer enjoys an improved profit margin.

Proponents argue that such proves that management is willing to put their money where their mouth is!

Incentives Summary
There are a number of serious issues that have to be managed if one chooses to use monetary safety incentives. One of these is the tendency for the monetary incentives to become "owned" by the employees as part of their wage. All effort should be utilized to avoid this possibility. Were a company to install monetary incentives company-wide on a basis that was not very difficult to attain, and if they kept these in place for some years the fact is the incentives will become part of the working conditions and can easily become viewed as owned by the employees. In a union represented workforce this can become a bargaining issue.

Equity, employee to employee, becomes an issue in the administration of any incentive program that is not totally equal in how it rewards employees. Equity is an employee morale issue thus must be watched and managed to minimize this problem.

My Personal View
It is mandatory that any incentive programs be preceded by an aggressive drive to bring the safety program into compliance with world class safety technique content. This should include the results of the Construction Industry Institute's Zero Injury research.

Otherwise a safety incentive program based on the lagging

indicator of worker injury will drive some injury reporting underground. After all, employees do want the bonus money and some will be tempted to get it by not reporting injuries.

On more than one occasion I have heard of cases where employees have gone to their own doctor after hours and paid out of their own pocket the costs of an injury rather than reporting an injury and causing all their working colleagues to lose the safety incentive.

Counterbalancing this, I have also heard of employees who were injured at home but brought the claim to work and alleged the injury occurred at work. In such cases incentives will somewhat curtail this inclination!

But on balance these under-reporting issues give rise for me to caution "would be incentive embracers" to wait until your zero injury safety culture is in place. Then if used, use incentives only on projects where they can be managed and safety personnel are on-site to assist in insuring injuries get reported.

Some Achieve Zero Injury through Extraordinary Skill
In support of those opposing monetary incentives there is something to be said for those who achieve Zero Recordables without monetary incentives.

Getting to Zero Injury through years of dedication of resources and the application of high levels of people management skills occurs in some companies. Many of these do not use monetary incentives. However they do involve their employees in the management of workplace safety and routinely recognize them for their achievements. There are major and some minor corporations that have been able to achieve the "Zero Recordable" injury level.

Extraordinary skill in human relations is always found to be a vital ingredient in these cases. If the worker truly feels a part of the effort of the corporation, worker's "vested interest" level increases and safer work occurs. Another thing that is "always" present in these companies is a passionate zeal for safety on the part of the Company Owner or the Chief Executive Officer.

Item 3 - The Zero Injury Safety Techniques Explained

1. Demonstrated Management Commitment –

Restated from Chapter 5
The key research finding was: <u>In the zero lost workday injury companies the CEO always had a key operating safety expectation placed before the company management.</u> It is paraphrased as follows -

> "It is my desire that we will do our work without injury to our employees. My belief is that all injury can be prevented and it is my expectation that there be no worker injury in our facilities or on our projects. If an injury does occur it will not be viewed by me as an acceptable event! And I personally will be involved in determining in what ways management failed in allowing the injury to occur.
>
> We will not set goals for injury! Our commitment is to ZERO Injury! This is not to be a statistics management effort. Rather our commitment shall be a complete devotion to the elimination of situations where our employees are at-risk or through education bring our employees to realize that any unsafe behavior is not solicited nor desired. I urge all employees, management and workers alike to willingly become partners in our commitment to eliminate employee injury."

In Chapter 12, I offer a prioritized plan that leads off with management taking action. Further, in the 2001 CII research, the task force developed additional measures. These are shown below. These give specifics on how to insure that top management's participation is routinely applied in a productive manner.

With each CII technique the Recordable Incident Rate results

for the contractors using, versus those not using these techniques are given.
These are:
1. Top management participates in investigation of Recordable injuries.
   - Participates in every injury – RIR = 1.20
   - Participates in 50% or less – RIR = 6.89

2. Company President/senior management reviews safety performance record.
   - Yes – RIR = 0.97
   - No – RIR = 6.89

3. Frequency of home office safety inspections on the project.
   - Weekly/Bi-weekly – RIR = 1.33
   - Monthly/Annually – RIR = 2.63

Creating a Zero Injury work place culture is an initiative that must be led by top management. To delegate this all-important activity to lower levels of management sends a signal that such a culture is not that important. With that signal the implementation effort is severely hampered.

2. Safety Staffing

There is a battery of information within the construction industry from those that are successful in achieving the Zero Injury performance which indicates that ratios of employees to Safety Specialists should not exceed 100. The CII 2001 research reported that ratios of 50 to one is common on very large projects where zero injury is the performance norm.

It will be no surprise if some in management wonder how a company can afford such a heavy contingent of safety professionals and specialists?

The answer is in two parts:

The first is: Many managers who are successful in achieving Zero Injury performance find such performance brings with it so much more than just a safety result that they cannot see the ratio being otherwise. They feel this way because they see the profound connection between safety excellence and reduced cost/schedule that they are convinced that operating in the Zero Injury culture produces the highest return on the investment. In these companies safety is of paramount importance and the staff is required to be in compliance with all company and regulatory requirements, and to guarantee that people are available to insure the highest quality in employee orientation and training.

The second is: The proper ratio for each company is obviously heavily dependent on the nature of the work each employer is doing. The 50 to one ratio was found in the large construction projects and large construction firms where employee turnover is very high. Smaller firms in the construction arena that have less turnover will require less safety staff with firms that experience little employee turnover having the highest ratios.

Remember this, the proper ratio is merely that required to insure all personnel receive quality in safety orientation and in safety training. Add to this the requirements for OSHA compliance, safety inspections and audits, the general maintenance of safety processes and procedures and you have near the correct number of safety personnel.

It is a given that the safety personnel you do have must be sold on the Zero Injury process and devote their creative skills to developing quality training and orientation materials for the employees.

3. Safety Training
Pre-Project/Work Safety Planning
"Weeks" before the start of a new production effort or project, the leaders, including any contractors get together to determine and discuss the various safety hazards the parties will encounter as the work progresses. The word "weeks" is

used to reflect the need to allow ample advanced planning in order that arrangements and coordination time is allowed for the parties to arrange for equipment and special tools to be acquired prior to the work requiring them. The point is that the Pre-Project Hazard analysis be held sufficiently in advance to allow for any planning that might result to be executed in a timely manner.

Attendance at this meeting should include all affected parties including Safety Representatives from any participating contractors and sub-contractors. Ample time should be allowed to go over all the aspects of the work to be done from beginning to end. Ample time for the meeting should be allocated to avoid appropriate safety planning from being deferred to a later date, due to the lack of time.

Pre-Task Safety Planning

Pre-task safety planning is a safety tool to be used by the foremen and the crafts. It is not difficult to do. It is so simple in approach that the biggest threat is that your people will think it a trivial matter. Do not be deceived. Pre-Task Safety Planning is a VITAL ingredient to achieving a Zero Injury working culture.

The most successful use it formally through the design of a form to be used by the foremen each and every time a task assignment is changed or given, and it is never used on a lesser frequency than each morning.

Typically those that use forms make them into a simple checklist that serves as reminders of the "at-risk" behaviors to be avoided on the tasks and to make work plans for task execution. When foremen and crew make these "pre-task plans", they serve as coordination for the execution of the work.

Those who use the pre-task planning process warn that if

during the execution of the work the execution sequence is altered, stop and make a new plan. For, they say, injuries frequently occur when changes are made without proper input and knowledge of all involved. It is OK to change the plan. Just do so formally. Stop and make a new plan.

The testimony of those who use the pre-task planning process is that their crews are more productive, leading to work completed ahead of schedule and on or under budget. These two aspects of Pre-Task Safety Planning are the reasons you will want to insure complete and total utilization of the technique.

4. Safety Training and Education
Safety Orientation

Safety Orientation of all new employees before they commence work is the objective. After all have been given the orientation covering the logic behind the Zero Injury commitment on the part of management, the effort then becomes centered on the new employee. Each new employee receives safety orientation prior to reporting to his/her foreman for a work assignment. It is during this orientation that the new employee learns about what it means to work in a culture where Zero Injury is the expected and supported norm of operation. Thorough safety indoctrination on the zero injury safety culture of the employer is the objective.

Know that each new employee comes to you as one who may have never heard of anything like what you are working to achieve: the completion of an entire year or project without an injury to any employee. Therefore the first thing that has to happen in orientation is this new way of thinking and working has to be explained in-depth ending with the new employee being asked to become an employee committed to working safe.

Defining what Zero Injury means in worker terms and the logic behind this concept must be presented. Doing this will help to "sell" the new employee on being a committed and participating member of the zero injury effort.

Also it will be appropriate to show the worker the various safety videos that can be a part of the new employee orientation. Videos on tool usage safety, behavior expectations, etc., are in order. But never rely just on videos for proper orientation. The number of employees attending is not critical as long as the facility is comfortable and the orientation session is varied to maximize the attendee's chances of absorbing the information.

In the ideal construction scenario the Orientation should open with the Owner Representative and the Project Manager giving a few brief remarks about their own commitment to safety. In a manufacturing situation it is desired that a member of management open the session. Then in either case the orientation presentation is turned over to the instructor designated to give the orientation. This can be anyone who has a passion for zero injury and basic presentation skills. Never allow an orientation to become a ho-hum process that lulls the new employees into a state of boredom.

Many companies use Safety Personnel to conduct the orientation, others use line management personnel. While the person used can be largely a function of availability, never use someone who is not gifted in the art of presentation and can display a passion about the subject of employee safety.

Time allocated for new employee Zero Injury orientation across industry varies from one to eight hours. My idea is that more than three hours is appropriate and more than a passing effort to provide the new employee all the information needed to become a participating member of the zero injury effort must be made.

The sessions can also include safety training in critical areas where appropriate. Among these could be the use of fall protection gear, respirators, and certain special tools with the latter being more trade specific.

Once again be careful to put all foremen through the same safety orientation that the crafts go through. The other option, which I have found in more than one instance, is not a pretty thing to contemplate. That would be sending new employees out to their foremen without the foreman having a clue as to what they have been told in orientation. Despite the obvious nature of the need to give foremen orientation it still happens that I find facilities and projects where the foremen have inadvertently been omitted from orientation.

Safety Training
In the 1993 CII research, when the researchers asked the crafts people what they thought was most important in achieving zero injury they answered with the following six primary items.
1. Fall Protection
2. Pre-Task Safety Planning
3. Safety Person on the job
4. Safety Training
5. Protective Training
6. Recognition and Incentives

Notice that two of the items are on training. The crafts personnel wanted Safety Training and specifically training on Personal Protective Equipment. Some of this can come during the safety orientation before reporting for work. Other training should come throughout an employee's time with the company. Today many companies give their employees training in OSHA compliance, CPR and First Aid training. Some even give an OSHA 10 Hour course. In the research when the researchers asked "How much time do you spend in Training?" the answer averaged 15 hours per year per employee. This is equivalent to two eight-hour shifts.

5. Worker participation and involvement

There are a number of methods available that allow the critical worker participation in the effort to achieve a Zero Injury culture. There are two, however, that are most effective. Both these are discussed at length in the body of this work. These are "Behavior Based Safety" (see Chapter 6, 10, 12) and "Safety Teams." (See Chapter 16, 17 and the appendix Safety Team articles.)

The former (BBS) is likely more suitable to rapid turnover workforces while the latter (Teams) is more suitable to situations where turnover is rather low.

6. Recognition and Rewards

This is a very critical item and many do not give it enough attention. For your employees to remain loyal to the Zero Injury effort it is very important to routinely give them recognition for worthy achievements in avoiding injury. Typically an employer is looking for significant improvement. It is critical that as this improvement occurs that the employer have ready an appropriate safety award with which to recognize a safety performance milestone. Obviously if an award is to be given soon, as in immediately upon achieving the milestone, some planning and award acquisition has to take place before the milestone is reached. I urge you to accomplish this preparation in a timely manner. It is very discouraging for the employees to know they have achieved a laudable and praiseworthy milestone, only to see management remain silent and as far as they can see inactive in preparing for recognition activity.

Remember research has found that "praise" is second only to money in motivating employees to excel.

Some employers find it appropriate to recognize the absence of Zero Lost Workday Cases as the first milestone then move this recognition to Zero Recordables as the performance continues to improve.

Regarding the question of worthiness. When is an achievement in eliminating injury worthy of recognition?

Here I strongly urge employers to keep historical data and use the national averages in the appropriate industry as your guide as to when to make an award. One easy milestone and usually a difficult one to achieve is when the employees have worked 200,000 hours with zero recordable injuries. This is equivalent to 100 employees working one year without an injury. That is the definition of Zero Injury when considering OSHA Recordables. On the BLS/OSHA base of 200,000 hours the achievement of zero recordables is the objective.

After this the objective becomes a repeat of the same achievement as many times as you can. The record as far as I know is repeating this 200,000-hour record back-to-back over 12 times in the construction industry. That is equivalent to over 2,400,000 recordable free hours worked. Some 97 recordable injuries avoided when compared to the national average for construction! Amazing!

If at the beginning you find your employees for the first time ever achieving 200,000 hours with no Lost Workday Cases, I have seen many employers make an award using this milestone. Then when the achievement improves to 200,000 hours with no recordable injuries they make the award even more significant.

Caution, do take a look at your industry and avoid making awards for safety achievements that are in fact mediocre or slightly better than average. Remember you are looking for zero, so be careful to give your awards based on this objective.

7. Contractor/Subcontractor management

This item applies to General Contractor's management of sub-contractors. However, the same emphasis is made for facilities in managing the contractor workforce that you retain to work in or on your facility.

Safety management usually begins with your own workforce. Soon after implementing the zero injury effort for your own direct hire employees it is timely to begin to work with the contractors who work for you to steer them toward the zero injury concept. The aim is that over time you will only retain contractors to work for you that have the same devotion to the zero injury effort as you do.

There are some legal implications and these can easily be avoided. I am not an attorney so do check with your legal advisor here. Typically a purchaser of a contractor's services cannot legally and should not be directly stipulating how the contractors you "have retained" should manage their safety program.

However the method that is typically legal in most states and municipalities for private work is to set the standards contractors have to meet to be considered as potential bidders on your work before you retain them. In the area of safety you simply state what the safety program requirements are for a contractor to qualify to bid your work. If the work is for a government body there is often an open bidding requirement so this will govern. If possible encourage the body seeking the bids to make some requirement in the area of safety. Such an effort is politically challenging and takes time.

Another aspect of working with a number of other contractors where the safety performance of any one impacts others is that it is highly productive to hold contractor's safety coordination meetings at least weekly but more often in highly congested areas.

8. Accident/Incident Reporting and Investigation
There are four parts of this area, 1. Tending to the injured, 2. Reporting the injury, 3. Investigating the injury and 4. Managing the injury.

1. Tending to the injured.
Primary in any injury situation is the proper care of the injured employee. The foreman must immediately arrange appropriate medical care as dictated by the extent of the injury. This can include the foreman transporting the employee to treatment/ medical care. If another supervisor or the safety person is available, these may assist or in some cases take over the care-giving role.

2. Reporting the injury.
Part of a Zero Injury culture is the specific accountability of "line management" to act as the primary means of insuring proper medical care is given as well as the communication link to top management when injury occurs. The reporting begins immediately with the foreman reporting to the second supervisory level.

The second level supervisor must be informed as soon as practical. First priority is always giving primary attention to tending the injured employee. This initial report may be delegated to a peer employee or another foreman in the area. Upon being informed the second level supervisor's immediate obligation is also to the injured to insure that all appropriate resources are made available to insure rapid care of the injured as dictated by the nature and severity of the injury.

Once care is assured, notification of the third supervisory level is timely. With today's high-tech communications capabilities reporting can be by cell-phone or radio. The object is that the injury notification reaches the top management within hours, if not minutes, after the injury.

3. Investigating the injury.

As soon as the injured party receives appropriate medical care the investigation of the accident leading to the injury begins immediately. This means no later than the day of the injury even if the injury occurs late in the workday. Injury to an employee justifies those involved in the investigation to work overtime if need be to get the process started. Delay in investigation allows needed details to slip away.

Every employer should have a pre-selected accident/injury investigation team always on alert in case there is a need. These personnel know in advance they are responsible to begin the investigation immediately. In a manufacturing facility the team members are appropriate leaders and safety personnel. Any technical support should be added as required. Line management should lead this investigation. This is part of the accountability aspects of safety in the workplace. Even if the injured employee's foreman is still tied up with tending to the injured the investigation can begin.

ALERT: This is a fact finding investigation aimed at understanding cause and effect, NOT a session to determine who is deserving of some kind of discipline for violating some safety code. Any contemplated punishment should take a back seat to the getting the facts. An injury investigation team should not be the group who determines appropriate disciplinary action. This aspect of an accident belongs to line management, not the investigating team.

First priority is to make a list of witnesses and co-workers in the immediate area. Then an investigation strategy is developed; first things first etc.

Too many times such responsibilities are "handed off" to the safety department. This is not appropriate. Management has the most to learn with the primary objective being to prevent a similar accident or injury due to the lack of swift and decisive management intervention. However, safety must always be represented on the team.

4. Tending the injury and the injured.
If the injury requires a medical professional or physician there are four management considerations that need attention. These are: a. Pre-selected care-givers and facilities, b. Employee communication as to who and where these facilities are located with phone numbers and maps, c. Responsible company personnel in attendance at the facility interfacing with the care-givers, d. Post injury management.

    a. It is always a good idea to pre-select from the local area medical professionals those you will use in caring for any injured employees. Interviews with these professionals outlining your priorities: of course the first of these is that your employee receive the finest care available. The second is to assure the professional that you are not trying to intervene in the appropriate care of the injured employee. That you are there for counsel on the nature of the employee's work, work-place and any alternate work that may be available in case the injured is placed on limited duty. That you also are here to assist the injured's family members in tending to their loved one.

    b. Employee communication as to who and where these facilities are located with phone numbers and maps.
All supervision should have printed information, phone numbers and maps on the location of care facilities and medical personnel that are pre-selected.

c. Responsible company personnel in attendance at the facility interfacing with the care-givers. This can be the foreman or other supervisory personnel. It also can be the safety person in some situations, however to delegate this important activity to the safety person dilutes the line management accountability, so it is not recommended as the norm.

d. Post injury management
If an injury is severe enough to require time away from work there should be a coordinated company wide process that continues to assure the injured receives proper medical care as well as routinely remains in contact with the injured in a care-giving mode. Such a mode is important to impart to the employee the sincerity of the employer regarding the injured employee's well-being and recuperation. As appropriate return to work possibilities are also discussed. Return to work is determined by the medical care-giver's advice to the injured and the employee's department as to available limited duty work opportunities, if needed.

Part of the post injury management process is to be actively engaged with the Workers' Compensation insurance carrier to insure the case is managed to your standards and your areas of concern for the care of your employee is given attention. It is always a good practice to be involved with the carrier's loss manager to discuss appropriate reserves for injuries requiring extended care.

9. Drug and alcohol testing

Most enterprises today utilize some sort of Drug Testing Program. Some of these are very good and some, for a number of reasons, do not go far enough to insure a drug free working environment. There are three desired features of a

Drug and Alcohol Testing Program. These are; 1. Pre-Employment Testing, 2. Random Testing, and 3. Post Accident Testing.

1. Drug Testing: A well thought out Drug Testing policy should be a part of every company that embraces the Zero Injury Concept. During the past decade the Drug Testing industry has expanded to where there are a number of qualified laboratories to handle the testing of specimens.

Pre-employment screening is mandatory in my view. On saying this I know a few companies who by policy do not allow their employees to be tested for reasons of personal privacy. This of course is their right. Utilizing such a company may give rise to other policy considerations by Owners or General Contractors.

The subject gets complex with legal implications so I will not offer comment other than to say your policy is your policy and their policy is their policy. If your policy says testing is required you do not have to employ a company that is not of like mind and purpose. There are likely exceptions again where municipal work is the object. Be aware that some local governments by statute do not allow drug testing even on private work within jurisdiction.

2. Random Testing: It is my belief that random drug testing is a vital part of a drug policy. While there are many examples of testing policies where random testing is not done, the best of policies do include such testing. The object of course is to discourage as much drug use as feasibly possible.

To not random test is to know that on any given day some numbers of your employees are sufficiently affected by the previous evening's drug use to be a danger to themselves and those that work around them. There is reluctance on the part of some Unions to allow random testing of represented employees. This is argued as a personal right of the employee to be free from invasive inspections into their personal habits.

On the other hand some Unions operate their own testing programs with some having random testing as a part of the Union's own policy. In other instances, particularly in the construction industry, where there is a policy of no random testing that this provision is waived by the Union when the Owner of the project requires random testing of all contractor employees.

3. Post-Accident Screening: Post accident drug testing is a productive policy feature. To not drug test after an accident is to omit an obligation to your employees who are drug free. Their safety is your immediate concern and often accidents do occur as a result of drug use. There is only one way to know: test.

The Zero Injury Guide Book

Item 4 - Zero Injury Return on Investment

Following is an explanation of the Return on Investment calculation for the installation of the Zero Injury Initiative.

Following I will detail describe the calculation row by row. Also see the spreadsheet at the end of this explanation.

Row 1   alpha and Information
R2   Title & Data
R3   Data
R4   Data
R5   Data
R6   Data
R7   Data
R8   Year
R9   Workers' Comp Premium Estimates
R10 Trend of EMR – Experience Modification
R11 Total Losses
R12 Losses due to Lost Time Injuries
R13 Losses attributable to pure Recordables
R14 Losses attributable to miscellaneous claims that were not classified as OSHA Recordable.
R15 Total number of claims
R16 Number Claims from Lost Time Cases
R17 Number Claims from pure Recordables
     Note: Rows R16 and R17 make up your total OSHA injuries.
R18 Number claims not OSHA rated
R19 Average loss per lost time case
R20 Average loss per pure recordable
R21 Average loss non-OSHA claim
R22 Estimated Productivity improvement from pre-task Planning
R23 Dollar value of productivity improvement

R24   Salary cost of any added safety staff
R25   Added cost of an eight hour safety orientation for each employee
R26   Added cost of zero injury safety training
R27   Cost of time to do pre-task safety planning
R28   Miscellaneous - such as awards and recognition costs
R29   Total costs of zero injury implementation
R30   Indirect cost factors (factor x direct costs = indirects)
R31   Indirect cost of lost time injuries (factor 2.08)
R32   Indirect costs of pure recordable injuries
R33   Total indirect costs
R34   Section title (ROI Basis loss savings)
R35   Sum of Costs (losses and indirect costs)
R36   Savings calculated off base year R35
R37   ROI
R38   Section title (ROI Basis premium savings)
R39   Sum of Costs (premium + indirects)
R40   Savings calculated off base year R39
R41   Return on Investment

The spreadsheet example follows. The example, Figure 1, uses a company with 100 employees with above average injury rates as shown on the sheet. The example also uses an average wage of $25 per hour and assumes an employee attrition of 20% per year. In the Zero Injury initiative we adopt an eight hour zero injury new employee orientation plus forty eight hours per year of safe skill and general safety training for all employees. These two features are aimed at employee education about the zero injury concept and insure they have all the necessary safety skills to achieve a zero injury work product.

The sheet takes into consideration the time it takes to do Pre-task Safety Planning and assumes a productivity improvement as the techniques becomes more effective with time.

Two approaches are used to calculate ROI. The first uses Injury Losses plus the indirect costs of injury. This applies more often when an employer is heavily insured and the injury rates are above OSHA National Average. The second approach uses Workers Compensation Premium plus indirect losses. This is more typical for many employers.

Notice that sometimes the ROI will begin on a negative in the first year (not atypical) and then improve year by year as injuries decrease until year 5 when ROI in the example hits 385%. As users of this calculation gain experience they will be able to fine tune the spread sheet to reflect their own numbers and injury frequency improvements. From the beginning take the example format and as the years pass just plug in your actual numbers to get the real ROI results.

The user should recognize that experience has shown that upon implementing the Zero Injury Concept in your company, if a company begins at the OSHA national average injury rates for their industry it will take from five to eight years to reach world class performance.

Figure 1 in MS Excel format reflects rows and columns where the calculation is made.

I have used typical direct costs of Lost Time Cases where the employee is given work as soon as the doctor agrees. If a return to work policy does not exist then these costs are typically much greater. On "pure" recordables I used typical real number of $600 that I see often my clients experience for "medical only injury cases."

Figure 2 contains a calculated data summary from Figure 1, for your ready reference.

The Search for Zero Injury

	B	C	D	E	F	G	H
1							
2	ROI Calculations	Hrs per year worked per employee =				2000	BeginEMR= 1.20
3		Number of emloyees		100	Manual Rate=======>		$12.00
4	Miscellaneous claim cost ======>>	30000	Turn over =	20.00%	Average loss of LT ===>		50000
5	Training time hrs per employee per year ============>>				48	Avg loss of Recordable=>	600
6	New Employee orientation time hrs ============>>				8	hr workdays per year=>	250
7	* calculated using 20 minutes a day if	0.333	AvgWage==	$25.00	Cost non OSHA claim		15000
8		$720,000	= <--WC Premium = MR x Wage Rate x employees x hrs per year x EMR				
9		Base Year	Yr 1	Yr 2	Yr 3	Yr 4	Yr 5
10	Premium Trend basis EMR =	$720,000	$600,000	$540,000	$480,000	$420,000	$360,000
11	EMR trend	1.20	1.00	0.90	0.80	0.70	0.60
12	Total losses	453,600	353,600	302,400	221,800	141,200	0
13	LTC losses	300,000	200,000	150,000	100,000	50,000	0
14	Pure Recordable losses	3,600	3,600	2,400	1,800	1,200	0
15	Misc claims losses	150,000	150,000	150,000	120,000	90,000	60,000
16	# Total claims	17	15	12	9	6	2
17	# Claims LTC	6	4	3	2	1	0
18	# Claims Pure Recordable	6	6	4	3	2	0
19	# Claims non-OSHA	5	5	5	4	3	2
20	Avg loss per LTC	50,000	50,000	50,000	50,000	50,000	50,000
21	Avg loss per Pure Recordable	600	600	600	600	600	600
22	Avg loss non OSHA claim	15,000	15,000	15,000	15,000	15,000	15,000

ROI - Figure 1

22	Productivity Improvement	0	0.01	0.02	0.03	0.04	0.05
23	Productivity Improvement $$ value	0	50,000	100,000	150,000	200,000	250,000
24	Added cost of staff	0	65,000	65,000	65,000	65,000	65,000
25	Added cost of orientation	0	4,000	4,000	4,000	4,000	4,000
26	Added cost of training	0	24,000	24,000	24,000	24,000	24,000
27	Pretask safety planning*	0	208,125	208,125	208,125	208,125	208,125
28	Misc added costs;I.e., awards	0	0	0	0	0	20000
29	Total costs-implementation 24->29	0	301,125	301,125	301,125	301,125	321,125
30	Indirect Costs of Injuries	LTC direct x 2.08		2.08	Recordable x 1.16		1.16
31	Indirect cost of LTCs - zero in year 6	624000	416000	312000	208000	104000	0
32	Indirect cost of Recordables	4176	4176	2784	2088	1392	0
33	Total indirects - assumed zero in yr 6	628176	420176	314784	210088	105392	0
34	**ROI Basis Savings on Injury Losses**						
35	Totals Costs R11+R29+R33	1,081,776	1,074,901	918,309	733,013	547,717	321,125
36	Savings reduced injury R36 d39-e39		6,875	163,467	348,763	534,059	760,651
37	Return on Investment =	0	2.28%	54.29%	115.82%	177.35%	236.87%
38	**ROI Basis Workers' Comp Premium Savings**						
39	Costs R10+R30+R34 Base year	$1,348,176	$1,020,176	$854,784	$690,088	$525,392	$360,000
40	Savings		$378,000	$593,392	$808,088	$1,022,784	$1,238,176
41	Return on Investment =	0	125.53%	197.06%	268.36%	339.65%	385.57%

ROI - Figure 1 continued

The Search for Zero Injury

Summary below of the Spreadsheet above

Cost of injury

	Premium	IndirectCost	TotalCost	Saved/yr
BaseYr	$720,000	$628,176	$1,348,176	0
Yr 1	$600,000	$420,176	$1,020,176	$328,000
Yr 2	$540,000	$314,784	$854,784	$493,392
Yr 3	$480,000	$210,088	$690,088	$658,088
Yr 4	$420,000	$105,392	$525,392	$822,784
Yr 5	$360,000	0	$360,000	$988,176

Cost of Implementation of Zero injury for 100 Workers

Year	Add Staff	Orient/Train	PretaskPlan	TotCost
BaseYr	$0	$0	$0	$0
Yr 1	$65,000	$69,000	$208,125	$342,125
Yr 2	$65,000	$69,000	$208,125	$342,125
Yr 3	$65,000	$69,000	$208,125	$342,125
Yr 4	$65,000	$69,000	$208,125	$342,125
Yr 5	$65,000	$69,000	$208,125	$342,125

Productivity improvement from Pre-task safety planning

Year	%Prod.Imp	Prod. Imprv
BaseYr	0	$0
Yr 1	0.01	$50,000
Yr 2	0.02	$100,000
Yr 3	0.03	$150,000
Yr 4	0.04	$200,000
Yr 5	0.05	$250,000

Overall Return on Investment

Year	Lower Cost DueTo Lower Injury	Savings Due ToImproved Productivity	Zero Injury Total Savings	Zero Injury Total Costs	Percent ROI +n34/o34
BaseYr	0	0	0	0	
Yr 1	$328,000	$50,000	$378,000	342,125	110%
Yr 2	$493,392	$100,000	$593,392	342,125	173%
Yr 3	$658,088	$150,000	$808,088	342,125	236%
Yr 4	$822,784	$200,000	$1,022,784	342,125	299%
Yr 5	$988,176	$250,000	$1,238,176	342,125	362%

Comments
This ROI calculation is a proforma presentation and shows the procedures used to make the calculation. You may wish to add in capability to reduce the outcome by present value and inflation factor considerations.

ROI - Figure 2

The Zero Injury Guide Book

REFERENCES:

Buchanan, Don, Editor, 2000, *"Zero Injuries Handbook,"* Hazard Alert Training & Supplies Canada, Inc.

Bureau of Labor Statistics, U.S. Department of Labor, *"Injury Incidence Rates for Construction,"* December 2001

Bureau of Labor Statistics, U.S. Department of Labor, *"Injury Incidence Rates for Manufacturing,"* December 2001

Business Roundtable, *"Improving Construction Safety Performance,"* the Construction Cost Effectiveness Project. A-3, New York, NY 1982

Business Roundtable Construction Committee: Construction Industry Safety Excellence Awards, New York, NY, 1987

Business Roundtable, *"The Workers' Compensation Crisis: Safety Excellence Will Make A Difference,"* New York, NY, 1991

Bureau of Labor Statistics, U.S. Department of Labor, *"Industry Injury Incidence Rates,"* December 2001

Construction Industry Institute, Austin, Texas: *"Zero Injury Techniques,"* Product 32.1 of the Zero Accidents Taskforce, Nelson, Emmitt J., Principal Author, 1993

Construction Industry Institute, Austin, Texas: *"Zero Accident Techniques,"* CII Source Document 86, Roger W. Liska, David Goodloe and Rana Sen, Clemson University, January 1993

Construction Industry Institute, Austin, Texas: *"Zero Injury Economics,"* CII Special Publication 32.2, Nelson, Emmitt J., Principal Author, September 1993

Construction Industry Institute, Austin, Texas: *"Indirect Cost of Injury,"* CII Product of Research Taskforce, Jimmie Hinze, University of Washington, Seattle, 1991

Construction Industry Institute, Austin, Texas: *"Making Zero Injuries a Reality,"* CII Product of Research Taskforce, Jimmie Hinze, University of Florida, Gatesville, 2002

The Zero Injury Guide Book

Curtis, Steven L., January 1995, *"Safety and Total Quality Management,"* Professional Safety

Flanders, Marc E, & Lawrence, Jr., Thomas W., December 1999, *"Warning, Safety Incentive Programs are under OSHA Scrutiny,"* Professional Safety

Geller, E. Scott, October 1997m *"Key Process for Continuous Safety Improvement –Behavior Based Recognition and Celebration,"* Professional Safety

Geller, E. Scott, October 1996, *"The Truth About Safety Incentives,"* Professional Safety

Krause, Thomas R. 1997, *"The Behavior Based Safety Process, Managing Involvement for an Injury Free Culture,"* Second Edition

Krause, Thomas R., 1998, *"Safety Incentives from a Behavioral Perspective – Presenting a Balance Sheet,"* Professional Safety

Levitt, Raymond E. and Samelson, Nancy M., 1993, *"Construction Safety Management,"* Second Edition

Nelson, Emmitt J., March 2002, *"Zero Injury Performance,"* Hydrocarbon Engineering

Nelson, Emmitt J., December 1998, *"Safety Commitment Redefined,"* Professional Safety

Nelson, Emmitt J., January 1996, *"Remarkable Zero-Injury Safety Performance,"* Professional Safety

Nelson, Emmitt J. & Haggard, Rusty, January/February, 1995, *"The Economics of Zero Injury,"* CFMA Building Profits

Nelson, Emmitt J., July 1995, *"A Shift is Afoot,"* Readers Pulse Section, Professional Safety

Nelson, Emmitt J., May 1994, *"Task force says use of safety techniques helps achieve "Zero injury,"* Professional Roofing

Peterson, Dan, January 1997, *"Behavior Based Safety Systems – A Definition and Criteria to Assess,"* Professional Safety

The Zero Injury Guide Book

Sims Jr., Bill, April 1999, *"Successful Safety Incentive Programs,"* Professional Safety

INDEX

INDEX

A

Accident Investigations -
  - near misses recorded? – 75
  - top management involved – 72
Accident review team -
  - established – 65
Accountable for injury/safety -
  - design accountability model – 85
  - hold managers – 85
  - line management – 85
Act of God -
  - Cause injury – 14
Alcohol - see Drug Testing
  - abuse program – 33, 65
  - test – 35, 71, 90, 190
American Industry -
  - pursuing safety excellence – 10
  - safety culture – 39
Analysis -
  - in-depth – 14
At-Risk behavior -
  - a leading indicator of injury – 77
  - a list is used – 77
  - careless act lessens – 39
  - chance taking – 77
  - no longer OK – 39
  - unacceptable to leaders – 77, 78
  - willingness to use – 77

Attitudes -
  - friendly – 105
  - improved with zero injury – 61
  - management – 135
  - mental – 171
Audits -
  - for BBS – 77
  - loss run – 50, 89
  - safety – 133
Author -
  - admits injury occurs – 38
Automatic safety progress system -
  - a proven system – 92
  - integrated system – 91
  - installation takes time – 92
  - needed – 92
  - operational guidelines – 101, 114
  - progress – 92, 93, 96, 97, 99, 100, 102
  - push start button – 127
  - reduces injury – 91
  - steps to – 95, 101, 116
Average -
  - Arithmetic – 10
  - Injuries – 11
  - some below average – 18
Awards -
  - for improved performance – 84

INDEX

B
Base year -
  - use of in ROI explained – 51
Behavior -
  - at-risk – 10, 13, 77, 78, 102, 105
Behavior based safety -
  - all management trained – 74
  - helped lower injury rates – 42
  - management embrace – 89
  - methods of incorporation – 78
  - observations made – 74
  - training given – 74
  - videos and software available – 78
  - worker to worker observations – 78
  - workers involved? – 78
Believing -
  - a status quo problem – 20
  - zero injury date – 29
Bidding -
  - more competitive with zero injury – 40
Bottom line -
  - pure gold to – 48
Business plan -
  - injury harms – 16
Business potential -
  - achieved through zero injury – 60
Business Roundtable -
  - attention helped reduce injury – 42
  - CISE award – 32
Buy in of all -
  - workers must – 38, 62, 66, 72

C
Case management -
  - difference in how – 44
  - employees back to work – 44
CEO -
  - Air Products – 32
  - believes in zero injury – 16
  - commitment – 24, 60
  - empowers employees – 67
  - gets report of injuries – 25, 83
  - gets routine safety reports – 78
  - intense passion needed – 82
  - knows safety statistics – 75
  - no injury acceptable – 24
  - on same footing – 60
  - recognizes zero injury annually – 84
  - sets expectation – 37, 67
Chance taking - See "at-risk" behavior
  - not OK – 39

Chemical Industry -
  - Gulf Coast region safety – 40
Commitment -
  - allows working together – 26
  - analogies – 58
  - are we committed in fact – 57
  - beyond superficial – 57
  - corporate – 27, 37
  - defined – 57, 58, 59, 60
  - definitions explored – 58
  - eliminates field argument – 25
  - gradual progress – 38
  - leaders lead – 24
  - little sleep if injury occurs – 82
  - represents a range of actions – 58
  - social meaning – 58
  - to zero injury unrealistic? –17
  - walking the talk - 38, 82
  - Webster definition – 58
  - zero injury definition – 60, 62
  - zero injury from sub-contractors – 84
Communication -
  - about the zero injury initiative – 53
  - all know about zero injury – 84
  - inter-employee – 86
  - leaders on zero injury – 24
Company leaders -
  - setting goals for injury – 24
Competitive edge -
  - with zero performance- 41
  - zero injury gives – 26
Construction -
  - hazardous – 29, 63
Construction Industry Institute -
  - 1988 research indirect costs - 48, 49
  - 1993 Zero Accidents Taskforce – 35
  - at University of Texas – 63
  - attention helped lower injury – 42
  - members injury rates down – 43
  - model off research results – 51
  - new task force in 1999 – 69, 70
  - new task force in 1999 – 65, 66
  - research – 35, 66
  - use 1993, 2001 research – 85
  - zero injury research – 34
  - zero injury techniques – 33
Continuous Improvement -
  - taking action – 87
Contract requirements -
  - set zero injury terms – 67
Construction Projects -
  - research done – 63, 70

203

The Zero Injury Guide Book

INDEX

Continuous safety improvement -
  - keeps program before employees – 83
Contractors -
  - Cherne – 30
  - Day and Zimmerman – 30
  - Fluor-Daniel – 30
  - S&B Engineering – 30
  - Winway, Inc. – 33
  - Zachry – 31
Corporate -
  - leadership required – 37
  - zero injury expectation – 23
Corporate Safety Committee -
  - agenda is changing the culture – 89
  - develop an agenda – 89
  - establish first – 89
  - regular meetings – 89
Cost of injury -
  - average in construction - 46
  - charged to departments – 84
  - concern about – 61
  - determine average cost – 44
  - gathering for ROI calculation – 52
  - helped reduce injury – 42
  - increased – 42
  - indirect costs recognized – 42
  - lower cost with zero injury – 41, 42
  - zero injury more important – 26
Co-workers -
  - do not want an injury to occur – 20
Culture -
  - change – 36
  - create ownership – 67
  - evaluating safety culture – 75
  - platform needed – 23, 60
  - that accepts injury – 16
  - zero injury – 23

D

Data sets in research -
  - time on safety – 63
  - use of 170 common techniques – 63
  - what hourly workers thought – 63
Delegating safety leadership -
  - top management directs – 82
Detailed planning -
  - inadequate time given – 61
Direct injury costs -
  - case management affects – 45
  - driven by actual costs – 45
Drug testing -
  - Alcohol – 65

  - policy – 71, 90, 190
  - post accident – 65
  - program content – 190
  - required – 71

E

Employees -
  - a valuable asset – 104
  - accept ownership of zero injury – 67
  - are treated – 102
  - attitude – 61
  - awards monthly – 84
  - begin to believe – 24, 40
  - commitment – 60
  - empowered by CEO – 67
  - get first day safety orientation – 84
  - hear commitment from leaders – 83
  - injured return to work – 45, 49
  - injuries costs money – 123
  - long term – 130
  - must "buy-in" – 38
  - nature of – 107
  - not badgered – 25
  - not ok to take risks – 39
  - rarely injured – 92
  - recognition for achievement – 84
  - safety needs – 25
  - safety training - 49
  - see progress – 78
  - sold on zero injury – 58
  - set own goals – 110
  - testimony – 29
  - trained in safety and BBS – 53, 78
  - turnover situations – 98, 110, 119, 129
  - workers know – 40
Employee conflicts -
  - provide resolution process – 121
  - recognize existence – 122
Employee involvement -
  - ask for voluntary – 100
  - productive ring to it – 126
  - with safety teams – 89, 90, 94
Employee relationships -
  - use role descriptions – 121
  - work out problems – 121
Employer -
  - does not want an injury – 20
  - sets expectation – 40

Engineering News Record -
  - top 400 contractors – 71

204

INDEX

Enthusiasm -
- for zero injury – 50

Environmental -
- compliance procedure – 114

Evergreen safety progress -
- employee help required – 96
- management system missing - 91
- needed – 91

Examples -
- commitment – 26
- leading in zero injury – 24, 29, 31

Excellence -
- achieved through zero injury – 39
- progress toward – 38
- safety excellence definitions varies – 10

Expectation -
- corporate – 25
- for zero injuries – 37, 40
- setting zero vital – 66

Experience Modifier - (EMR)
- explained – 46
- formula – 46
- high EMR costly – 46
- how used – 46
- low EMR an advantage – 46

Environmental -
- compliance procedure – 109

F

Fallacy -
- to think injury cannot be prevented – 15

First aid cases -
- measure hours between? – 19

Foremen -
- foremen set safety action goals – 115
- pre-task safety planning – 61
- push production – 60
- train – 65

G

Goal setting for some number of injuries -
- a look at commitment and goals – 64
- a mistake to set injury goals – 21
- employees believes injury OK – 23
- goal setting problems illustrated - 18

Goals - safety -
- "bottom up" process – 110
- chronology is important – 111
- guidelines – 111
- guidelines illustrated – 116
- guideline on content – 116
- no injury goals – 110
- review frequency – 113
- team leaders lead – 115

Good news -
- injury prevented –15

H

Hazards -
- analysis – 64
- early analysis – 66
- elimination not guaranteed – 67
- industries different, people same - 12

Hinze, Dr. James W. -
- researcher for CII task force – 70

Hours worked -
- between injuries – measure? – 20

Humanitarian considerations -
- safety driven by - 61, 62

I

Implementation of Zero Injury -
- critical priorities – 79
- of zero injury techniques – 24

Incentives -
- based on zero injury – 74
- family members involved? – 74
- formal program? – 73
- many oppose – 86
- see appendix E – 144
- sometimes deceptive – 85
- type of incentives – 65
- use in interdependent mode –85
- written program – 65

Indirect costs -
- hard numbers from CII – 50
- loss in efficiency – 50
- multipliers – 56
- used in ROI calculation – 54

Indoctrination to Zero Injury -
- through safety training – 51

Injury -
- calculating the average costs – 46
- calculating the total costs – 48
- cost of – 45, 46
- doubters feel injuries will occur – 21
- is not OK in goal setting – 22
- is preventable – 58
- millions of hours worked without – 19
- not tolerated – 25
- prevention esteemed – 25
- steadily declined – 42, 43
- unacceptable - 24, 25, 58, 61, 82

205

INDEX

Injury cost -
- average calculated – 49
- considered – 48
- direct and indirect – 123
- higher than we think – 123
- indirect ratios to directs given – 48

Injury frequency - See OSHA
- lagging indicator – 86

Injury investigations -
- specifics covered – 63, 64

Injury management -
- assign responsibilities – 89
- decide injury investigation process – 89
- design a program – 89
- develop physician liaison protocol – 89
- develop return to work policy – 89

Injury prevention -
- interventions – 14
- will occur 13

Injury rates, OSHA -
- down over decade of 1990 -1999 – 43

Injury reporting -
- incentives can deter –86
- immediate – 83
- important – 65
- to CEO – 83

Injury statistics - see OSHA
- work hours reported – 65

Insurance carrier -
- discounts – 48
- doesn't insure profits lost by injury – 68

Integrated safety management system -
- approach to managing safety – 88
- integrates skills of workforce – 89
- not a theory – 92

Integrity -
- in record keeping – 29

K

Key point -
- Mind source of failure/mental safety – 12

L

Labor leaders -
- increased attention to safety – 42

Lagging Indicators -
- worker injury frequency – 77

Leader -
- make changes carefully – 136
- of teams - see Appendix
- set expectations – 127
- team leaders – 129, 132
- top management – 135
- verbal support – 133

Leadership - safety -
- contains five elements – 24
- contains integrity – 24
- delegating responsibility – 83, 85
- initiatives – 84

Leading Indicators -
- Zero at-risk behavior – 77

Line Management -
- held accountable for safety – 83

Liska, Dr. Roger -
- ran zero injury research - 33, 63

Logic -
- against setting injury goals – 21
- flawed logic – 21
- logic behind zero injury concept – 19
- zero injury logic proven – 27

Losses -
- CII research – 50
- from injury – 50
- loss run source of information – 50

Lost time injuries -
- average cost – 52
- measure hours between? – 19
- overseas record – 31
- site visit by management – 82

Lost workday cases -
- research basis – 63

M

Machine failure -
- cause injury – 14

Magazines -
- Engineering News Record – 71

"Making Zero Accidents a Reality" Task F. -
- 2001 report out – 70
- zero recordable injury investigated – 70

Management -
- actions in harmony – 39
- actions parallel talk – 38
- attention increases with cost – 46
- commitment - 24, 57, 72, 78, 88
- delinquent if uninterested safety – 52
- devotion to zero injury – 66
- does not want an injury – 20, 59
- evaluated on safety – 75, 76, 77, 84
- integrated teams – 90, 91, 94, 126
- investigating injury – 72
- of injury – 89
- lives in a "glass house" – 133
- meetings begin with safety – 83

206

INDEX

- proactive – 114
- quality role – 124, 125
- relationships – 121
- reviews of goals – 113
- safety alignment needed – 88
- safety foundation – 103, 104
- safety management choices – 98, 99
- safety management process – 91, 92, 93, 94, 96, 97, 99, 109, 126
- safety management system – 91, 92, 101
- safety toolbox – 97, 100
- speaks out on safety – 133
- strategy – 126
- subcontractor – 90
- system evolution – 91
- team safety – 89, 90
- trained in BBS – 78
- visit to site of injury promptly – 83
- walking the talk – 25
- workers given to recognition – 84

Managers -
- enlightened – 10

Managing safety -
- involve employees – 38
- with people – 11

Mathis, John -
- Chaired CII Task Force 2001 – 70

Mission statement -
- includes safety vision – 103

Money -
- where mouth is! – 24

Monetary support -
- for safety – 24

Motivation -
- Motivational challenge – 21

N

National injury average -
- has improved – 27
- injury free days – 27
- not exceeding – 53

Near hits/misses -
- investigated – 65
- reporting encouraged – 75
- tracked – 75

Nelson, Emmitt J. -
- Chair of Zero Accidents Task F. – 63

New Employee Safety Orientation -
- specifics – 65

O

Orientation -
- all workers attend formal – 73, 75
- every worker receive? – 73
- on first day for new employees – 83
- on safety – 65
- owner involved – 65
- project specific – 65

OSHA -
- 200,000 hr. OSHA base explained – 17
- compliance costs in base year – 53
- helped reduce injuries – 42
- investigates incentives – 85
- statistics – manufacturing – 17

OSHA Recordables -
- Zero achieved – 52

OSHA/BLS – injury frequency -
- construction rate – 57
- manufacturing rate – 57
- rate for 2001 – 47
- recordable rates improved – 34
- remarkable records – 28, 29
- tables tell story – 43, 44
- workhours between injuries – 13

OSHA/BLS versus CII members -
- tables reflect progress – 43, 44

Overseas safety data -
- records – 30

Owner -
- Air Products – 32
- CITGO – 30
- Chevron - 40
- Shell Chemical – 30
- involvement important – 66, 68

P

People management -
- a safety issue – 12

Performance evaluations on safety -
- for all employees annually – 84

Petro-chemical industry -
- led progress – 40

Planning safety – see pre-task planning
- gets job done more effectively – 61
- safe production – 99

Premium for Workers' Compensation -
- formula – 47

Pre-project safety planning -
- early hazard analysis – 66
- meetings held – 75

Pre-task safety planning -
- are meetings held? – 73
- improved safe production – 61, 99
- meetings held – 75

207

INDEX

- safe details – 64
- Priority -
  - safety is number one – 25
- Pro-active safety -
  - develop safe procedures – 119
  - from reactive – 114
- Problem -
  - in not achieving zero injury – 20
- Production -
  - from good relationships – 123
  - improves with zero injury – 83
  - management of – 92
  - psychology of – 122
  - pushing production ruled – 88
  - safe production – 99, 75
  - safety has priority over – 83
  - safety not a production problem – 25
- Productivity -
  - improved with zero injury - 41, 88, 99
  - not lowered by safety – 88
- Profit -
  - anticipated result of business – 104
  - increased - 62, 113
  - key question raised – 60
  - off of injury not wanted – 103
  - mention in guidelines letter – 104
  - profit lost by injury not insured – 67
  - profit margin discussed – 60
  - quicker way to increase? – 48, 61
  - zero injury more important – 26
  - zero injury protects – 124
- Projects -
  - zero accident research used – 43
- Pure costs -
  - of recordable explained – 84
- Purpose of Zero Injury research -
  - show how to achieve – 63
  - to convince management – 63
  - to identify techniques – 63

Q

- Quality -
  - circles - 99, 109
  - important – 67
  - in safety – 125
  - non-quality costs money – 123
  - of effort required for zero injury – 67
  - Philip Crosby - 127
  - revolution – 124
  - what about - 124-125

Quality Leaders in America -
  - Crosby – 124
  - Deming – 124
  - Juran – 124
  - "Zero Injury" term from Crosby - 124
- Questions -
  - how to get started? – 35
  - how zero injury achieved - 33, 35
  - 6?

R

- Realistic -
  - zero unrealistic – 38
- Recognition and rewards -
  - family members of workers attend – 74
  - formal worker incentive program 74, 166
  - group performance focused – 84
  - routine means developed – 84
  - safety recognition monthly – 74, 82
  - use – 84
- Recommendations -
  - the critical – 82
- Recordable -
  - measure hours between? – 19
  - work millions of hours between – 19
- Record keeping -
  - games people play – 29
- Records -
  - leading examples – 30, 31
- Relationships productive -
  - spell out desired in mission – 102
- Research -
  - 1993 research conducted – 33, 35
  - 2001 research – 70
  - findings – 33, 34, 35, 64, 65
  - indirect cost – 50
- Research, applied results-
  - recordable rates dropped – 34
- Research recommendations -
  - Listed – 67, 68
- Responsibility -
  - line management – 84
- Return on Investment - ROI
  - base year discussed – 52
  - brilliant investment – 52
  - calculation explained – 54, 55, 56
  - in zero injury – 50
  - payout high – 52
  - questions regarding – 50
- Risk taking - "see at risk"
  - a rare event – 12

S

Safe environment -

208

The Zero Injury Guide Book

INDEX

- desired – 105
- desired workplace norms – 105

Safety -
- at the expense of profit? – 60
- leadership – 24
- mental – 12
- planning important – 73
- psychological game – 12
- revolution – 27
- safety staffing ratios – 72

Safety Associations -
- ASSE – 42
- helped lower injury rates – 42
- National safety Council – 42

Safety Audits -
- off site personnel conduct – 77

Safety Consultants -
- push for zero injury – 74

Safety culture - see zero injury culture
- document – 103
- getting help – 107

Safety excellence -
- achieving – 39
- BRT CISE awards – 33
- defined – 10
- recognized – 32, 33

Safety goals -
- bottom up goals – 90
- defining safety goals – 90
- employees set own – 110
- for technique implementation – 90
- goals calendar – 116
- guidelines letter – 127
- how to set – 111, 112, 116
- leader influence – 114, 115
- lower teams do goals first – 115
- reviews – 113, 114, 116
- technique implementation – 112
- work related – 115

Safety incentives - see "incentives"
- re-addressed – 54

Safety management -
- Zero injury Concept – 15

Safety management system -
- integrated – 91
- foundation – 101
- make a choice for teams – 99

Safety Meetings -
- all meetings begin with safety – 83
- held – 75
- tail gate meetings – 73

Safety mission statement -
- create or alter – 102
- your foundation – 102

Safety performance -
- 30 times better than average – 18, 19
- mediocrity – 11
- step change in improvement – 68

Safety personnel -
- a staff function – 85
- advisors/auditors only – 83
- compliance & training focused – 83
- head called Director – 85
- important – 62
- ratio safety staff to workers – 72
- report to head office – 75
- staff to needs – 84

Safety planning -
- pre-task/project - 90, 115, 116

Safety plans -
- site specific plan exists – 77

Safety procedures -
- development – 24

Safety Procedure Manual -
- create – 119
- given to those needing – 120
- kept current – 120

Safety process -
- institutionalize basic process – 67
- uses 170 techniques – 67

Safety program -
- broad program essential – 66
- contain essential techniques – 66
- have an innovative – 83

Safety progress -
- evergreen - 109
- need it now – 126
- process – 91
- will come quickly – 128

Safety reports -
- routine and frequent – 83

Safety roles -
- understanding – 131, 132, 133

Safety statistics -
- average – 11
- comparing – 11
- normalized – 11
- zero injury – 32

Safety Surveys -
- perception surveys conducted – 73

Safety teams -
- a process to "Zero Injury" – 91
- agenda is safety management – 90
- choices have to be made – 98, 99

The Zero Injury Guide Book

INDEX

- develop at lower organization levels – 91
- each have prioritized action plan – 90
- help process – 109
- link teams with organization – 89
- long term process – 95
- many questions answered in index – 95
- team goal setting – 112, 113, 115, 116
- vary in sophistication – 110

Safety tools -
- integrated system – 91
- pre-task planning – 180
- recognition – 167
- safety management tool box – 97, 100, 126
- teams a tool – 130
- what to use next – 126
- worker involvement – 77

Safety training -
- at least four hours per month – 73
- avoid at risk behavior – 10
- behavior based safety – 89
- formal – 85, 115, 116
- safety staff – 133

Saudi Arabia -
- safety records – 31

Schedule -
- employees not badgered – 26
- risk taking unacceptable to meet – 82
- zero injury more important – 26

Senior Management -
- reviews safety reports – 75

Shell Oil Company -
- cost of Workers' Comp – 4
- fatality cause – 14

Skeptics -
- doubt zero achievable – 17

Status quo -
- do not accept – 20
- setting goals for injury – 20

Sub-contractors -
- active participants – 72
- manage safety – 90
- require well run safety programs – 84
- required to comply – 74
- required to submit safety plans – 75
- sanctioned if not in compliance – 74

Successful companies -
- in construction – 11
- in other industries – 11
- records set – 30, 31, 32, 33

Substance abuse testing -
- alcohol and drugs – 65

Supervision -
- evaluated on safety? – 74
- not badgering employees –26
- training on safety – 73

Supervisor -
- found production improved – 61

T

Task Force of CII -
- Making Zero Accidents Happen – 35, 69
- Zero Accidents – 33, 63

Team leader -
- lead in goals development – 90
- linked organizationally – 89
- sets performance standards – 111
- sharing information – 105, 132
- team leader functions – 112, 113, 115

Tenacious -
- leaders to get to zero injury – 24

Training – Safety
- conducted? – 73
- for foremen and superintendents – 83
- in safe work habits – 85
- paramount importance – 13
- safety training is vital – 38
- spend more time in – 53
- training is budgeted – 74
- training time specified - 71

Tucker, Dr. Richard –
- Founding Director CII – 5, 33

U

Universities -
- Clemson University – 33
- CII at University of Texas – 63
- University of Florida - 70
- University of Washington – 196

Unsafe behavior - See "at-risk"
- avoided – 37
- disappears – 39
- free of – 88

V

Vision -
- for zero injury – 24
- newly found – 53

W

Walking the talk -
- by recognition – 84
- CEO/COO – 82
- corporate commitment – 38

210

The Zero Injury Guide Book

INDEX

Whatever it takes -
- will do to prevent injury – 16

Workdays -
- between recordable injuries – 27

Workers - see "Employees" also
- commitment – 57
- found production improved – 61
- injury unacceptable – 82
- involvement – 71
- must be sold on zero injury – 53
- must "buy-in" – 38
- research asked their opinion – 64
- trained in BBS – 77

Workers' Compensation -
- attention to coverage – 47
- audit loss runs monthly – 89
- avg. manual rate for construction – 46
- close cases quickly – 89
- cost passed on to owner – 41
- loss run – 49
- maintain carrier interface – 89
- premium formula – 46
- underlying costs – 48

Worker's family -
- do not want an injury – 21

Worker participation in safety -
- involve BBS – 89
- safety teams – 89

Workplace -
- injury free – 57

World class -
- defined as no injuries – 52
- ROI significant – 50
- safety performance – 18
- trendsetters – 29

Z

Zero Accidents Task Forces -
- chartered – 63
- findings – 34, 35
- findings used – 45
- Making Zero Accidents a Reality – 35, 69
- research – 33
- purpose – 63

Zero Injury -
- accepted norm – 39
- adopt philosophy – 67
- all work at zero some hours – 18
- ask the workforce for – 27
- believing you can – 13
- commitment to – 60
- defined – 17
- improves production – 78
- more likely achieved – 67
- not a theory – 56
- obviated by setting goals – 23
- possible – 16, 17
- research of – 33
- search for – 10

Zero injury concept -
- embraced – 51
- discovered by contractors – 60
- invented by contractors/owners – 16
- logic behind – 19
- means no injuries – 17
- reached critical mass – 39

Zero injury culture -
- 24 point evaluation – 75
- a change in culture – 13
- change the – 88, 89
- through employee involvement – 91
- very profitable – 123
- zero injury - 82, 88, 90, 93, 94, 98, 99 100, 101

Zero Injury data -
- three data sets taken – 63, 64

Zero injury practitioners -
- found job effective – 61
- more profitable effort – 61

Zero injury process -
- cost of implementing – 53
- embracing – 51

Zero Injury Research -
- conclusions listed – 66
- findings – 64, 71
- in detail – 63, 70
- in summary – 32, 36
- showed quality very important – 65
- specific techniques used important – 66

Zero Injury Responsibility -
- line management – 83

Zero Injury techniques -
- five base techniques in 1993 – 64, 65
- nine techniques found in 2001 – 71
- relative impact given – 72
- sub-techniques - 66, 67
- use incentives last – 85

Zero Lost Workday Cases -
- achieved by large and small – 66
- research base in 1993 – 63

Zero Recordable -
- American record – 13
- becoming reality – 35, 70
- being achieved – 34, 70

211

Printed in the United States
124850LV00006B/7-45/A